MOONWALK THE UNTOLD STORY OF MICHAEL JACKSON

Unveiling the Secrets, Struggles, and Triumphs of the King of Pop

JAMES N PATEL

"MOONWALK THE UNTOLD STORY OF MICHAEL JACKSON"

"Unveiling the Secrets, Struggles, and Triumphs of the King of Pop"

By

James N patel

All rights reserved. No part of this publication may be reproduced, distributed, or transmitted in any form or by any means, including photocopying, recording, or other electronic or mechanical methods, without the prior written permission of the publisher, except in the case of brief quotations embodied in critical reviews and certain other noncommercial uses permitted by copyright law.

Copyright © JAMES N. Patel, 2024.

Table of Contents

INTRODUCTION

CHAPTER 1

The Jackson 5's Revolution: A Domestic Matter

Motown Superstar: Taking Center Stage

Moonwalk Chronicles

CHAPTER 2

Unconventional: Individual Goals and Musical Ventures

Revealing the Secrets of the Gloved One: The Thriller Phenomenon

Sales and Awards Above All Records: Unprecedented Accomplishments

CHAPTER 3

Character and Acting

The Silky Criminal Age: Sophisticating Performance Techniques

Taking on Difficulties and Accepting Change

CHAPTER 4

Dreams of Neverland

The Man in the Mirror: The Humanitarian Trajectories of Michael

Striking a Note: The Restorative Power of Music

CHAPTER 5

Obstacles and Successes

The Return of the King: This and Beyond

CHAPTER 6

Legacy of the Gloved One

Pop Culture Impact: Michael Jackson's Lasting Influence

Pop Culture Impact: The Lasting Influence of Michael Jackson

CHAPTER 7

Behind the Mask

The Mysterious Persona: Revealing the Individual Hidden Behind the Mask

Ties between family, friends, and confidantes in Neverland

CHAPTER 8

Michael's Business

Conflicts over contracts, copyrights, and other legal issues

Michael's Excursions Outside the Theater

CHAPTER 9

Symphony of Images

The Enchantment of Michael's Dance: Joint Ventures and Novelties

The Visual Extravaganza: Musicals, Tours, and Magnificent Exhibitions

CHAPTER 10

Tours That Never End: The Joy and Cost of Traveling Life

The Paparazzi Lens: Michael's Struggle with Invasion of Privacy of Michael Jackson

CHAPTER 11

Warm Remarks

Michael's Jackson parenthood

Emotional Lyrics: Interpreting Michael Jackson's Songs' Poetry

CHAPTER 12

Reflections by Moonlight

Moonwalk in Literature: The Influence of Michael on Books and Society

Reexamining Neverland: Documentaries and Posthumous Narratives

Life Guidance

INTRODUCTION

Greetings from your amazing adventure through the fascinating life of Pop's King! Prepare to moonwalk through the amazing highs and lows of a musical phenomenon as you turn the pages of Michael Jackson's biography. This literary journey extends an invitation for you to enter Michael's universe, where the rhythms are just as exhilarating as the dance floor under the stars.

You will read about the development of a young star who became a worldwide sensation on these pages. Experience the deep songs that defined an era, feel the heartbeat of his early Motown days, and taste the enchantment of the moonwalk. Beneath the dazzling glove and the recognizable fedora is a story of tenacity, inventiveness, and unwavering spirit.

Take in all of the tales that give his mysterious personality life. The visionary, philanthropist, and timeless performer behind the music is revealed in this biography, which features songs like "Thriller" with its contagious energy and "Man in the Mirror" with its deep reflection.

Come and join us on this literary stage where each page resonates with the beat of Michael's unmatched legacy and every chapter is a dance. Prepare yourself for an up-close look at the extraordinary life of a pop culture icon. As you embark on this trip, may the enchantment of Michael Jackson's narrative fill your heart and spirit!

CHAPTER 1

Rhythms of Childhood

The first years of a musical career

Michael Jackson started his musical career at an early age as a member of the Jackson 5, a Motown group he created with his siblings.

He was born in Gary, Indiana, on August 29, 1958. In the late 1960s, The Jackson 5 gained rapid notoriety, with Michael serving as the group's captivating leader and main singer. Early on, his remarkable singing abilities and charisma on stage were apparent, paving the way for his eventual success as a solo artist.

When Michael Jackson and the Jackson 5 released their first album, "Diana Ross Presents The Jackson 5," in 1969, at the early age of eleven, it included the smash ballad "I Want You Back." They shot to worldwide fame thanks to the song, which also launched Michael Jackson's legendary career. With follow-up singles like "ABC" and "I'll Be There," the group's chart-topping triumph persisted.

Even though they were very successful together, Michael always wanted to pursue a solo career. His first solo album, "Got to Be There," which he released in 1971, demonstrated his range and unique voice. The popular single "Title Track" demonstrated Michael's ability to enthrall crowds even while performing alone.

Michael Jackson's artistic development persisted throughout the years. His album "Off the Wall," which he co-produced with the renowned producer Quincy Jones, was published in 1979. An important turning point in his career was this album, which had an adult-oriented R&B vibe and a more mature sound overall. Hits like "Rock with You" and "Don't Stop 'Til You Get Enough" cemented Michael's reputation as a formidable solo artist.

Michael Jackson did, however, achieve previously unheard-of heights with the 1982 publication of "Thriller". The album achieved widespread recognition, shattering records and winning praise from critics. Not only did hits like "Billie Jean" and "Thriller" rule the charts, but they also completely changed the music business. The accompanying music videos demonstrated Michael's inventive use of visual narrative, particularly the ground-breaking "Thriller" video.

Michael Jackson persisted in pushing the limits of mainstream music throughout the 1980s. Hits from his albums "Bad" (1987) and "Dangerous" (1991) included "Smooth Criminal" and "Black or White." His distinct fusion of pop, rock, and R&B, together with his unparalleled dancing skills, catapulted him into global prominence.

Michael Jackson's influence expanded into philanthropic and humanitarian endeavors in addition to his musical accomplishments. He has had an enormous impact on the music business and popular culture, and he will always be remembered as a great character in music history. Even with the scandals that surrounded him in later life, Michael Jackson's formative years set the stage for a career that would permanently alter the mainstream music scene.

The Jackson 5's Revolution: A Domestic Matter

"The Jackson 5 Breakthrough: A Family Affair" describes a critical juncture in the legendary pop group The Jackson 5's career, which was fronted by the very gifted and youthful Michael Jackson. Their career took a new turn after the breakthrough, establishing them as one of the most important bands in popular music history.

The Jackson 5 were siblings Jackie, Tito, Jermaine, Marlon, and a baby Michael when they were first founded in 1964. The family trio attracted Motown Records' notice with their remarkable musical ability and harmonizing voices. The Jackson 5's signing with Motown in 1969 would turn out to be a crucial step toward their success.

Released in October 1969, "I Want You Back," the Jackson 5's breakthrough record, shot them to worldwide fame. The young voice and charismatic stage presence of Michael Jackson instantly won over the hearts of people all around the globe. With its number-one position on the charts, the song launched a run of singles that would characterize their early career.

Hits like "ABC," "I'll Be There," and "Never Can Say Goodbye" followed, showcasing the group's adaptability and Michael's growing vocal ability. One of their defining songs, "I'll Be There" went on to become their fourth straight number-one smash and demonstrates Michael's emotional depth and maturity beyond his years.

The Jackson 5's popularity was due to their collective energy as well as Michael Jackson's particular brilliance, which produced a distinctive sound that appealed to a wide range of listeners. The group's contagious enthusiasm and riveting appearances on shows like "Soul Train" and "The Ed Sullivan Show" helped to further solidify their reputation.

The Jackson 5's breakthrough success served as a springboard for Michael Jackson's later-legendary solo career. The family's harmonies and his amazing skill opened the door for later solo albums like "Off the Wall," "Thriller," and "Bad."

The film "The Jackson 5 Breakthrough: A Family Affair" pays tribute to the family's unwavering skill and their combined commitment to their work. Their impact on the music business is enduring, inspiring a new generation of musicians and reaching well beyond the Motown heyday of the 1970s.

The Jackson 5 continued to make important contributions to the music business after their first success. Their influence on pop culture disregarded age and racial distinctions, making them an international phenomenon. Among them, Michael Jackson stood out as a cultural figure who went above his position in the group to become known as the "King of Pop."

The Jackson 5 are unique in the music industry because of their dynamic fusion of pop, R&B, and soul. They left a lasting impact as they pioneered the way for upcoming boy bands and family acts. A variety of musical genres were included on the group's albums, which included "Diana Ross Presents The Jackson 5," "ABC," and "Third Album," which also showed the brothers' artistic development.

The Jackson 5's popularity extended beyond the music charts. Their animated series "The Jackson 5ive," which ran from 1971 to 1972, also had its imprint on television. This animated series, which captivatingly blended music and narrative, gave viewers a rare look into the Jackson brothers' life.

The Jackson family had difficulties throughout their rise to fame, such as disagreements with Motown about royalties and creative control. With their signing to Epic Records in 1975, the group embarked on a new phase of their career. By doing this, Michael Jackson was able to be close to his siblings while still pursuing his goals as a solo artist.

In the late 1970s and early 1980s, Michael Jackson's solo career took off thanks to hits like "Off the Wall" and the Grammy Award-winning "Thriller." The latter, which came out in 1982, is still the record with the most sales. Michael Jackson's avant-garde music videos, including "Thriller" and "Billie Jean," completely changed the way the music business looked.

The Jackson 5 continued to get together for rare performances, such as the Motown 25: Yesterday, Today, Forever television special in 1983, even as Michael Jackson's solo career took off. The Jackson family's timeless connection and musical brilliance were on full display throughout the reunion.

The Jackson 5 had a lasting effect on musicians of many genres, affecting even later generations of musicians. In addition to his artistic accomplishments, Michael Jackson's charitable work cemented his reputation as a world-renowned humanitarian. The family's turbulent but remarkable narrative is still ingrained in music history, having left a lasting impression on both the business and the hearts of millions of fans throughout the globe.

Motown Superstar: Taking Center Stage

Motown Marvel: Taking Michael Jackson's Place in the Sun

The term "Motown Marvel" describes Michael Jackson's incredible journey through the storied Motown record company, a crucial period in the King of Pop's brilliant career. Born in Gary, Indiana, on August 29, 1958, Michael Jackson became well-known as the lead vocalist of the Jackson 5, a group he established under the Motown label with his brothers.

Berry Gordy Jr.'s Motown Records, which he created in the late 1960s, revolutionized the popular music industry.

The label gained notoriety for its unique "Motown Sound," which was defined by smooth production, tight rhythms, and soulful songs. Michael Jackson led the Jackson 5 to rapid success as one of Motown's most renowned performers.

The trio shot to worldwide fame with the publication of their breakthrough hit, "I Want You Back," in 1969. Worldwide audiences were captivated by the group's contagious energy and Michael's captivating and passionate voice. The singles that followed, such as "ABC" and "I'll Be There," cemented the Jackson 5's position as Motown's biggest act.

Michael Jackson's solo career at Motown was likewise quite successful. Early solo releases, such "Got to Be There" (1972) and "Ben" (1972), demonstrated his flexibility and offered a glimpse of the unmatched solo career to come. But it was his exit from Motown in 1975—which signaled the end of the Jackson 5 era—that prepared the way for Michael's rise to prominence on his own.

In addition to perfectly capturing Michael Jackson's ascent to prominence inside the Motown family, Motown Marvel also captures the wider cultural influence of Motown Records in the 1960s and 1970s. With its collection of gifted African American musicians who found mainstream success, Motown was instrumental in dismantling racial barriers in the music business.

The groundwork for Michael Jackson's subsequent successes, such as his Grammy Award-winning album "Thriller" and his incomparable impact on pop culture and dance, was set during his tenure at Motown. Motown Marvel is proof of the mutually beneficial partnership between a budding superstar and a record company that shaped a time and had a lasting impression on the music industry.

Moonwalk Chronicles

Creating the Moonwalk: Dancing Steps That Characterized a Time

"Crafting the Moonwalk: Dance Moves that Defined an Era of Michael Jackson"

Often referred to as the "King of Pop," Michael Jackson had a profound impact on dance in addition to revolutionizing the music business. The Moonwalk is among his most famous dance steps that came to characterize a whole period. Let's explore the intricacies of how this captivating dance technique was created and how it came to represent Michael Jackson's extraordinary skill.

The moonwalk, often referred to as the backslide, is a dancing technique in which the performer seems to be sliding backward while moving forward. When Michael Jackson performed "Billie Jean" on the television program "Motown 25: Yesterday, Today, Forever" in 1983, he demonstrated this maneuver for the first time. The show captivated the attention of millions of people throughout the globe and was a revolutionary event in the history of dance and music.

Examining the Moonwalk's origins is crucial to comprehending how it was made. Even though Michael Jackson is often given credit for making the act famous, African-American dance is where the Moonwalk first appeared. Street dancers who used gliding and sliding motions in their routines, as well as tap dancers like Bill Bailey and Cab Calloway, were major influences.

Jackson, however, took these inspirations and multiplied them. He spent endless hours honing the Moonwalk, which combines deft footwork, precise timing, and an appearance of defying gravity. The seamless execution of the Moonwalk is proof of his painstaking attention to detail in both choreography and performance.

Shifting one's weight to provide the impression of forward motion while going backward is the secret to doing the moonwalk. Jackson developed a smooth glide by learning how to slide his foot backward while maintaining a forward body angle. His performances were characterized by their physical and artistic virtuosity, which called for an extraordinary sense of balance and control.

The Moonwalk evolved into a cultural phenomenon that went beyond its technical aspects. It came to symbolize not only a time but also Michael Jackson's creative persona. The routine demonstrated his creative approach to dancing and his ability to slickly combine many forms, such as modern street dance and classic tap.

The influence of the Moonwalk went much beyond the stage. It inspired a new wave of dancers, launching an international dance frenzy, and solidifying Michael Jackson's status as a dance legend. He made the maneuver a distinctive part of his shows, captivating audiences and establishing his place among the greatest performers of all time.

To sum up, the Moonwalk was painstakingly created by taking ideas from several dance styles and bringing them to a previously unheard-of degree of complexity. In addition to defining an era, Michael Jackson's commitment to mastering this famous technique had a lasting impression on the dance community, demonstrating his creative genius and permanently changing the face of popular culture.

CHAPTER 2

Unconventional: Individual Goals and Musical Ventures

Michael Jackson's pioneering album "Off the Wall" was released in 1979. It demonstrated his evolution from a young child star with the Jackson 5 to an experienced solo performer, and it was a pivotal moment in his career. The record is praised for its cultural influence and innovative music in addition to its financial success.

Musical Innovations and Style:

1. Genre Fusion: Pop, R&B, funk, and disco were among the genres that "Off the Wall" embraced. This diverse blend demonstrated Jackson's breadth as an artist.

2. Quincy Jones Collaboration:- The renowned Quincy Jones produced the record, beginning a fruitful partnership that would last until "Thriller." Jones had a major influence in creating the album's upscale sound.

3. <u>Disco Influence:</u>- Songs like "Don't Stop 'Til You Get Enough" and "Rock with You" clearly reference the late 1970s disco movement. These tracks were taken beyond the disco genre by Jones's production and Jackson's powerful vocals.

4.<u>Vocal Performances:</u>- Michael Jackson's expressiveness and vocal range were evident. His vocal expression of passion established a benchmark for pop musicians in the following decades.

5.<u>Songwriting Contributions:</u>- Jackson collaborated on a number of the album's tracks, demonstrating his developing songwriting abilities. This artistic engagement was a change from the more regimented setting he was in during his Jackson 5 days.

Business Achievement:

1. list Performance:- "Off the Wall" peaked at number three on the Billboard 200 list, a huge commercial triumph. Four top 10 tracks on the Billboard Hot 100 were also produced by it.

2. Ground-Breaking Accomplishments:- Being the first album to produce four consecutive No. 1 singles in the US from a single LP, the album broke records. Additionally, it was a global hit, enhancing Michael Jackson's standing as a superstar.

3. Critical Approval:- Reviewers applauded the album for its originality and Jackson's grown-up attitude. Its lyricism, general musicianship, and production value all garnered favorable reviews.

Cultural Influence

<u>Breaking Racial Barriers:</u>- The music business had a racial barrier breakthrough with Michael Jackson's "Off the Wall" popularity. He turned into one of the first Black musicians on MTV to have meaningful crossover success.

<u>Fashion and Style:</u>- Jackson's distinctive looks, such as his fedora and glove, came to define the time. Music videos that he directed, such as "Don't Stop 'Til You Get Enough" and "Rock with You," redefined the visual narrative genre.

<u>Legacy and Influence:</u>- Michael Jackson's "Off the Wall" served as a precursor to his subsequent hits, such as the revolutionary "Thriller." Pop, R&B, and dance music from later generations have been influenced by the album.

Michael Jackson's album "Off the Wall" continues to be a key release in both his career and the annals of popular music. The music business has been forever changed by its inventive sound, financial success, and cultural influence, cementing Michael Jackson's reputation as the "King of Pop."

Revealing the Secrets of the Gloved One: The Thriller Phenomenon

"The Thriller Phenomenon: Unveiling the Magic of the Gloved One"

Known as the "King of Pop," Michael Jackson had a lasting impression on the music business. His record "Thriller" is proof of his unmatched talent. When "Thriller" was released on November 30, 1982, it not only became the best-selling record ever but also ignited a cross-cultural craze.

- Musical Proficiency: The Thriller Tracks

There are nine songs on the CD, all of which highlight Jackson's creativity and adaptability. The ground-breaking music video for the legendary title track "Thriller," which was filmed by John Landis and featured Michael Jackson's trademark dancing routines along with Vincent Price's unforgettable narration, is well-known. Other notable songs include "Billie Jean," which not only topped the charts but also made the Moonwalk famous, and "Beat It," which has an incredible guitar solo by Eddie Van Halen.

- Creative Music Videos: Revolutionizing the Scene

The album's accompanying music videos were groundbreaking. Jackson transformed the medium into an art form via his partnerships with well-known filmmakers. The 14-minute "Thriller" video, in particular, demonstrated Jackson's devotion to visual narrative and precision. His dance routines—most famously, the zombie dance—became legendary and revolutionized the music video business.

- Cultural Impact: Dismantling Norms and Breaking Barriers

"Thriller" became more than simply a great song; it was a phenomenon in society. Jackson's ability to cross racial and cultural barriers was shown by the album's widespread popularity. His innovative music videos helped to dispel the prevalent racial prejudices in the music business and led to the broad acceptance of black musicians on MTV.

- The Perfect Performances of The Gloved One

The spectacle of Michael Jackson's live concerts was unmatched. His shows included the ideal fusion of dance, music, and dramatic components. Following the debut of "Thriller," he embarked on the "Bad World Tour," which demonstrated his ability to enthrall audiences everywhere. His trademark dances, like the Moonwalk, were iconic, and he had an enormous impact on musicians who came after him.

- Legacy: Beyond the Album

Years after its debut, "Thriller" is still influential in popular culture. Jackson's position as a significant figure is cemented by the album's influence on the music business as well as his charitable giving and humanitarian endeavors. Notwithstanding the issues that surrounded him, there is no denying his contributions to entertainment and music.

- Result: The Lasting Enchantment of the Gloved One

In addition to shattering records, Michael Jackson's "Thriller" expanded the boundaries of what an album might do. From its innovative music videos to its influence on culture, "Thriller" continues to be an unmatched phenomenon. The Gloved One has made a lasting impression on the entertainment industry with his ability to mix genres with ease, creative approach to music videos, and unwavering devotion to breaking down boundaries. As we ponder the enchantment of "Thriller," generations are still motivated by Michael Jackson's impact as a performer and cultural figure.

- The Studio Magic and Teamwork Behind "Thriller"

The careful production effort and teamwork that went into making "Thriller" are also responsible for its popularity. Michael Jackson collaborated extensively with the late great Quincy Jones, whose attention to detail and acute ear for musical arrangements brought the record to previously unheard-of levels. The collaboration between Jackson and Jones, in addition to the contributions of well-known musicians and composers, was essential in creating the musical masterpiece known as "Thriller."

Sales and Awards Above All Records: Unprecedented Accomplishments

In terms of sales, "Thriller" was a phenomenal success, shattering records that are still held today.

It was the first album to produce seven singles that were ranked in the top ten on the Billboard Hot 100. It was certified 33× Platinum by the Recording Industry Association of America (RIAA), meaning that more than 33 million copies were sold in the US alone. Globally, the record became the number-one album in many nations, ensuring Michael Jackson's place in history as a superstar.

"Thriller" received similarly remarkable critical acclaim, and in 1984 it broke all previous records by winning eight Grammy Awards, including Album of the Year. The album's continuous inclusion in rankings of the "greatest albums of all time" is proof of its lasting appeal.

- ❖ Statements of Fashion: The Classic Glove and Red Jacket

Beyond only music, Michael Jackson left a lasting impression with his wardrobe choices, which became icons. His red leather jacket from the "Thriller" video and the white glove with sequins he wore during concerts were defining characteristics of his image. In addition to enhancing the visual spectacle of his performances, these fashion statements also had an impact on 1980s fashion trends.

- ❖ Gifts to Charity: Cure the World

Millions of people were captivated by Michael Jackson's music, but his charitable endeavors also had a lasting impression. Songs like "Heal the World" and "Man in the Mirror" demonstrated his dedication to bringing about social reform and world peace. Jackson wanted to utilize his fame to effect good change, and his charity endeavors, which included establishing the "Heal the World Foundation," demonstrated this goal. His humanitarian legacy was added to his musical accomplishments.

❖ Eternal Impact: Inspiring Generations

The song "Thriller" has had a lasting impact on musicians and artists of later generations. The work of modern pop singers who recognize Michael Jackson's revolutionary contributions to the music business demonstrates its influence. The album's songs are often sampled, covered, and mentioned, demonstrating its continued significance in the current music scene.

❖ Final Thought: An Everlasting Event

In conclusion, "Thriller" is more than just an album—it's a timeless cultural icon. Michael Jackson's album smashed records and revolutionized the music business, showcasing his unmatched inventiveness, creative brilliance, and unwavering commitment to excellence. The "Thriller Phenomenon" is proof of the Gloved One's lasting power, guaranteeing Michael Jackson's legacy in music and culture will last for generations to come.

CHAPTER 3

Character and Acting

Captain EO to Bad: An Odyssey in Film and Music

A retrospective trip called "Captain EO to Bad: A Cinematic and Musical Odyssey" captures Michael Jackson's revolutionary career from the 1986 release of "Captain EO" to the landmark 1987 release of "Bad" album. "Captain EO" is a pioneering science fiction film that runs for 17 minutes and was created and directed by George Lucas and Francis Ford Coppola. It was Jackson's first attempt at 3D filmmaking and was made for Disney theme parks.

The main character in Michael Jackson's film "Captain EO" is the title character, who sets out to restore happiness and harmony to a dystopian planet under the control of an evil queen with a motley crew of space misfits. The movie combines inventive storyline, futuristic graphics, and Michael Jackson's trademark musical talent. Included are original tracks such as "We Are Here to Change the World" and the well-known "Another Part of Me," which demonstrate Jackson's skill at fusing storyline with music.

After "Captain EO" became successful, Michael Jackson started working on "Bad," his seventh studio album. When the album was released in 1987, it wasn't as catchy as its predecessor "Thriller," but Jackson's dedication to creativity was still evident. The classic singles "Bad" include "The Way You Make Me Feel," "Smooth Criminal," and "Man in the Mirror." Jackson's title as the "King of Pop" was cemented with this album, which also stretched the bounds of pop and R&B.

Martin Scorsese's "Bad," the title track's accompanying short film, is another example of Jackson's commitment to making visually arresting and captivating music videos. The movie tells the story of Jackson's encounter with Wesley Snipes' character, a gang boss, and urban kids street dancing. Jackson's unparalleled dancing skills were on display in the legendary dance routine at the subway station, which is still deeply ingrained in popular culture.

Michael Jackson's versatility is shown by the contrast between "Captain EO" and the "Bad" period, which skillfully combines his musical genius with dramatic narrative. These achievements not only highlight his impact on popular culture but also his dedication to pushing creative limits and making a lasting impression on the entertainment sector.

The Silky Criminal Age: Sophisticating Performance Techniques

Michael Jackson's career reached a turning point during the Smooth Criminal Era, which demonstrated his unmatched talent for performing. During the late 1980s, he released his classic album "Bad" in 1987, which included the immortal hit song "Smooth Criminal." This album came to define the period. Jackson cemented his title as the King of Pop during this period with his avant-garde dancing movements, inventive creative vision, and ground-breaking music videos.

The album "Bad" itself served as evidence of Jackson's development as a musician. He abandoned the Motown sound of his early work in favor of a more modern pop and rock sound, working with producers like as Quincy Jones to create a dynamic and varied musical experience. Especially "Smooth

Criminal," with its irresistible beat, memorable lyrics, and Jackson's distinctive vocal delivery, stood out.

However, the innovative music videos that accompanied the songs were just as important to defining the Smooth Criminal Era as the music itself. Jackson demonstrated his inventive use of visual effects in the "Smooth Criminal" short film, including the anti-gravity lean, a dancing motion that has come to be associated with him. The elaborate choreography and chic film noir style demonstrated Jackson's dedication to expanding the possibilities for music videos.

The Smooth Criminal Era was defined by live performances that enthralled audiences all over the globe in addition to the music and visuals. Jackson's performances during these concerts were an unmatched spectacle. His renditions of "Smooth Criminal" were the epitome of style and perfection, with his immaculate voice and deft execution of intricate dance moves.

Another distinctive feature of this period was the integration of theatrical components into his live performances. Jackson's concerts were immersive events that merged dance, narrative, and music, going beyond simple musical presentations. With his trademark white suit and fedora, Jackson's Smooth Criminal persona came to represent his capacity to create personalities that went beyond the confines of conventional performance.

Aside from his live performances, Michael Jackson became a well-known worldwide philanthropist during the Smooth Criminal Era. His humanitarian endeavors and support for children's hospitals and other philanthropic organizations gave his public image a more nuanced quality and revealed the entertainer's sensitive side.

For Michael Jackson, the Smooth Criminal Era was a time of transformation. It demonstrated his capacity to reinvent himself while keeping his own style and demonstrated his growth as an artist. The legacy of the period is still felt today; Jackson's influence continues to define popular music and performance, and "Smooth Criminal" is still a timeless masterpiece.

Michael Jackson had a huge impact on popular culture throughout the Smooth Criminal Era, in addition to his music and visuals. The "Smooth Criminal" music video's trademark black leather jacket, white hat, and anti-gravity slant became cultural icons, representing Michael Jackson's distinct aesthetic and unrivaled performance skills. Jackson's reputation as a fashion icon and musical pioneer was cemented during this time.

Jackson's influence was seen in the dance and choreography fields. The precise spins and gravity-defying leans in the "Smooth Criminal" music video established new benchmarks for dancing in the business. Jackson's pioneering methods were so popular that dancers and choreographers all over the globe tried to imitate him, solidifying his reputation as a dance industry pioneer.

Jackson's charitable endeavors also witnessed a surge during the Smooth Criminal Era. His devotion to having a beneficial influence outside of the entertainment industry was shown by his engagement in charity causes, such as his support for AIDS research and disaster relief. Jackson was a worldwide celebrity, but his commitment to charity at this time showed that he was also a socially aware person who used his power for the greater good.

In addition, Jackson reached a new height of commercial success with the release of the "Bad" album, which included

"Smooth Criminal." The album yielded many successful singles, including "The Way You Make Me Feel" and "Man in the Mirror," which strengthened his position as the number-one artist on the charts. Jackson's ability to relate to listeners from a wide range of backgrounds demonstrated the Smooth Criminal Era's music's international appeal.

The Smooth Criminal Era has cultural relevance outside of the West as well. Michael Jackson's worldwide influence broke down cultural barriers and across geographic borders, reaching audiences in Asia, Africa, and beyond. Few musicians had ever been able to contribute as much to the globalization of pop culture as he did; his music videos were highly anticipated and warmly received everywhere.

Michael Jackson's impact was evident in music, dance, fashion, and charity throughout the Smooth Criminal Era. It had a lasting impression on the entertainment sector, influencing how the next generations of artists treated performance, originality, and the use of visual aspects in their works. Fans are still moved and enthralled by the lasting impact of the Smooth Criminal Era, which cemented Michael Jackson's status as a musical icon.

Taking on Difficulties and Accepting Change

Known as the "King of Pop," Michael Jackson had many obstacles in his life and career, but he proved again and again that he could accept change and grow both emotionally and professionally.

Making the switch from being a kid star with the Jackson 5 to a solo artist was one of the early obstacles in Michael Jackson's career. Even with the Jackson 5's enormous success, Michael still had the difficult challenge of becoming a respected solo musician. But he not only conquered this obstacle but also laid the groundwork for his eventual domination in the music business with the publication of his album "Off the Wall" in 1979.

Jackson had difficulties throughout his career, including altering musical trends and evolving dynamics in the business. He embraced the new genre of music videos in the 1980s, redefining the format with hits like "Thriller." This demonstrated his flexibility in the face of shifting creative landscapes and cemented his position as a forerunner in the entertainment industry.

Michael Jackson faced difficult personal and legal circumstances in the 1990s, which put his fortitude to the test. He persisted in honing his art and creating music that connected with listeners all around the globe in spite of the difficulties. His album "HIStory: addressed the difficulties he encountered and confirmed his standing in the music business while also exposing a sensitive side of the artist.

Jackson's embrace of change extended beyond his music; during the years, he underwent a discernible physical transformation. Jackson openly disclosed that he had vitiligo, a skin disorder, and insisted that his shifting appearance was due to medical conditions rather than personal preferences, even as the media made assumptions about his changing appearance. His candor regarding his difficulties was a reflection of his dedication to sincerity and openness.

Even in the face of legal challenges and financial setbacks, Michael Jackson never stopped innovating. His posthumous album "Xscape" and his Las Vegas residency proved his continued influence on the music business even after his premature death in 2009.

Michael Jackson had many difficulties throughout his childhood, from overcoming personal and legal troubles to adjusting to life as a child celebrity. But his capacity to welcome change, try out novel musical genres, and adjust to changing conditions cemented his reputation as a legendary figure in the entertainment business. He showed fortitude, inventiveness, and an unshakeable dedication to his craft throughout it all.

Michael Jackson's path was not devoid of public scrutiny and controversy. The overwhelming media attention that surrounded his personal life—particularly his romances, family issues, and court battles—was one of the most prominent obstacles he had to deal with. Jackson was always under investigation, yet he was able to remain professional in public appearances, often drawing attention back to his charitable work and music.

In response to shifting social mores and attitudes, Jackson also tackled racism and social injustice in his songs. Songs like "They Don't Care About Us" and "Black or White" demonstrated his dedication to utilizing his position to spread themes of justice and harmony. His readiness to use art to address social concerns demonstrated his commitment to changing the world for the better.

In addition, Michael Jackson's charitable activities showed his empathy for other people. His engagement in a number of humanitarian endeavors, like as his backing of children's hospitals, HIV/AIDS research, and disaster relief, demonstrated his ambition to have an impact outside of the entertainment industry. He continued to make large donations to philanthropic groups in spite of financial difficulties, creating an enduring legacy as a humanitarian and musical legend.

The advent of the internet and the digital era during Jackson's latter years altered the way people listened to music. He adjusted in spite of these changes by looking into fresh distribution strategies and using technology to communicate with followers. His ability to function in the ever-changing music business demonstrated his progressive outlook and will to remain relevant.

Michael Jackson's life was a tapestry of hardships, conflicts, and victories. His standing as a versatile artist and cultural icon was cemented by his capacity to persevere in the face of hardship, his dedication to social concerns, and his flexibility in changing times. Beyond his creative output, one lasting legacy of Jackson is his willingness to accept change and utilize his position to further good deeds.

CHAPTER 4

Dreams of Neverland

Building Neverland: Michael's Dreamy Paradise

The book "Creating Neverland: Michael's Visionary Utopia" discusses Michael Jackson's grand idea to build an entertainment complex and utopian city. Jackson's idea came to life physically at Neverland Ranch in Santa Ynez Valley, California.

When Neverland Ranch was first built in 1988, it was meant to be the King of Pop's personal getaway. Inspired by the concept of an eternal childhood paradise and J.M. Barrie's Peter Pan, Jackson developed the land into a vast estate with a movie theater, zoo, and other attractions. Jackson intended to build a location where people may experience endless youth and pleasure, and the name "Neverland" symbolizes this wish.

There were rides, games, and other attractions at Neverland's amusement park, which created a whimsical environment. The property had a full-scale steam train that went around it, adding to the atmosphere of a storybook. A private zoo with exotic animals was another aspect of the property that highlighted Jackson's affinity for the magical world of Peter Pan.

Neverland was intended to be a haven for impoverished kids, not merely a private hideaway for Jackson. Jackson welcomed many youngsters from different nonprofit groups into his idyllic house. Children were able to spend a carefree day in a fantastic atmosphere and experience the enchantment of Neverland thanks to these visits.

Even with its original splendor, Neverland Ranch eventually faced financial difficulties and legal troubles. Jackson was the target of accusations that damaged his reputation and put a burden on his finances. When Jackson faced foreclosure in 2008, he gave up ownership of Neverland Ranch.

Michael Jackson's life and career are still deeply entwined with the memory of Neverland. It bears witness to his wish to establish a happy, innocent sanctuary where people may forget about the problems in the outer world. Even while Jackson may no longer be the proprietor of the actual Neverland, the idea and the memories connected to it remain a significant part of his legacy.

Michael Jackson's imaginative effort to realize an idealistic fantasy was the creation of Neverland. The ranch let kids experience the wonders of a fantasy world and served as more than simply a place for relaxation. Neverland Ranch continues to stand as a testament to Jackson's unwavering dedication to bringing pleasure and happiness to everyone, even in the face of difficulties and ownership changes.

The Man in the Mirror: The Humanitarian Trajectories of Michael

In addition to being one of Michael Jackson's most well-known songs, "The Man in the Mirror" also reflects his significant humanitarian impact. The King of Pop showed a strong dedication to changing the world over his career by addressing several international concerns with his wealth and notoriety.

Michael Jackson was a prolific philanthropist who supported many different organizations. He had a significant impact on the battle against HIV/AIDS, among other things. During the late 1980s, when the illness was still highly stigmatized, Jackson supported a number of nonprofit groups that worked to increase public awareness of and financing for HIV/AIDS research.

In 1985, Michael Jackson collaborated on the song "We Are the World," a charity record that included performances by several well-known performers. The song's revenues were donated to USA for Africa, an organization that was founded to help starving and sick African countries. In addition to becoming a universal symbol of togetherness, the song helped generate millions of dollars for charitable causes.

Apart from his involvement in healthcare issues, Jackson also had a strong interest in organizations that support children. In 1992, he established the Heal the World Foundation, whose goal is to enhance the lives of children everywhere. The organization funded a number of projects, including helping with relief efforts after natural catastrophes and supplying children in war-torn Sarajevo with medical supplies.

Michael Jackson's dedication to education was also shown by his donations to scholarship programs and support of groups like UNCF (United Negro College Fund). He thought that education could empower people and communities, especially those who were struggling financially.

Jackson remained a champion for constructive change throughout his life, even in the face of personal and legal obstacles. His song "Man in the Mirror" sent a strong message about introspection and the duty each person has to make a positive difference in the world. The song's lyrics beg listeners to change—beginning with themselves—in order to build a society that is more fair and caring.

Michael Jackson really wanted to change the world, as shown by his humanitarian impact. His support of several charity projects, from education to children's welfare and healthcare, demonstrates the breadth of his generosity. Jackson gained a reputation as one of the most significant and kind people in history because of his activism and music, which had a long-lasting effect on the entertainment business and the wider society.

Michael Jackson was not limited to making monetary donations in his charitable pursuits. He regularly participated in practical humanitarian work, often going to villages, hospitals, and orphanages to promote and raise awareness of the causes he was passionate about. He is distinguished as a real humanitarian by his sincere empathy and compassion for people in need.

Jackson concentrated his humanitarian efforts on children's hospitals, which was a noteworthy feature. He would go see ill kids, cheer them up, sign autographs, and spend time with them. His commitment included more than simply financial contributions; it involved building relationships with those going through difficult times.

Michael Jackson founded the Heal the World Foundation, which carried out many international initiatives. The "Heal L.A." project, which sought to enhance the lives of impoverished youngsters in Los Angeles, was one noteworthy endeavor. As part of the project, a children's hospital was built, and mentoring and educational initiatives were put in place to help underprivileged children.

Jackson was also a fervent supporter of environmental concerns. He enthusiastically supported programs aimed at conservation and sustainable living since he understood how important it was to protect the environment for coming generations. He utilized the money from the single to help environmental groups. His song "Earth Song" compassionately addressed environmental challenges.

Michael Jackson was always the first to provide humanitarian relief when things become worse. For instance, he made significant donations to relief operations and traveled to the afflicted neighborhoods to provide consolation and support during the 1992 Los Angeles riots. His commitment to bringing about positive change in the world was shown by his capacity to organize resources and leverage his famous position for the greater good.

Michael Jackson's dedication to charity did not waver in the face of scandals and personal difficulties. In addition to the millions of cash he contributed, his humanitarian impact is shown by the many lives he touched by his active participation and sincere concern for the welfare of others. His humanitarian work is still having an effect, and he continues to serve as an example to others who want to change the world for the better.

Striking a Note: The Restorative Power of Music

"Striking a Chord: Music as a Healing Force of Michael Jackson"
Through his legendary career, Michael Jackson, the King of Pop, not only had a lasting impression on the music business but also exemplified the deep healing power of music. Jackson's ability to use music to address social concerns and emotionally connect with audiences demonstrated the healing power of his artistic vision.

With the 1991 release of his album "Heal the World," Michael Jackson demonstrated the power of music as a healing force in one of the most prominent cases. Songs like "Black or White" and "Will You Be There," in addition to the title tune, conveyed sentiments of empathy, solidarity, and social duty. Jackson wanted to use these songs to motivate listeners to make a difference in the world and to promote good change.

The use of music as a therapeutic tool was also greatly aided by Michael Jackson's charitable activities. His commitment to a number of humanitarian causes and children's hospitals showed his conviction in the transformational power of music to uplift and comfort people going through difficult times.

Jackson's music often mirrored the personal hardships he had throughout his life, giving him a way to communicate with those going through similar experiences and convey his feelings. Songs like "Man in the Mirror" and "Heal the World" demonstrated Jackson's intention to encourage people to make changes in themselves that would result in a more understanding and peaceful society.

In addition to his socially aware songs, Michael Jackson's music provided many with a means of escape, providing consolation and comfort during trying times. His heartfelt melodies and contagious rhythms have the power to cheer people up and inspire happiness and optimism in the face of hardship.

Jackson made innovations in dance and visual narrative with his music videos, therefore his impact went beyond music. His ground-breaking music videos, including "Thriller" and "Smooth Criminal," went viral, enthralling viewers and offering a visual complement to the therapeutic themes present in his songs.

Michael Jackson's compositions serve as evidence of the therapeutic value of art. Jackson made good use of his position to influence people and society at large with his heartfelt songs, charity endeavors, and socially aware lyrics. His influence still motivates musicians and fans alike, highlighting the power of music as a catalyst for recovery and constructive transformation.

Beyond only his singles and albums, Michael Jackson's music had a profound therapeutic impact. His live performances were legendary, bringing pleasure and harmony to a broad range of fans throughout the globe. His explosive energy on stage had a transforming impact, enabling people to temporarily forget their problems and bond over music, which is a global language.

Furthermore, Jackson's distinct singing style and capacity to emote deeply via song struck a strong chord with listeners. Whether it was the unadulterated frankness in "She's Out of My Life" or the forceful affirmation of one's own value in "Bad," his music had the potential to arouse compassion and understanding and provide comfort to those experiencing tough times.

Jackson's versatility as an artist was shown by the 1982 record "Thriller," which went on to become the best-selling album of all time. The album's wide variety of genres—from pop to rock to funk—showcased his dedication to writing songs that would be liked by a wide spectrum of listeners. Because of its inclusiveness, his music was able to cure listeners from a wide range of socioeconomic and ethnic backgrounds.

Michael Jackson has had a significant effect on his followers' mental health. Numerous people have related personal tales of how his music helped them get through trying times. The tunes and lyrics provided a kind of catharsis and comprehension that cut over linguistic and cultural barriers, acting as a friend for those facing difficulties.

Jackson's support for initiatives that provide impoverished youngsters access to music and his advocacy for the value of arts education further demonstrated his conviction in the healing powers of musical expression. He showed his dedication to making sure that future generations might benefit from music's healing power by supporting these initiatives.

To put it simply, Michael Jackson's healing legacy extends beyond the money made by his records and the awards he won. It lives in the combined experiences of his admirers who were comforted, uplifted, and delighted by his music. Jackson made a lasting impression on the globe with his unmatched skill and dedication to good change, serving as a constant reminder of the powerful influence music can have on both the individual and societal healing processes

CHAPTER 5

Obstacles and Successes

Scandals and Conjecture: Handling the Media Upheaval

The King of Pop, Michael Jackson, was a well-known international figure who sparked controversy around his life in addition to his revolutionary contributions to the music business. Jackson's story was heavily reliant on scandals and rumors, which generated a media frenzy that often eclipsed his artistic accomplishments.

The early 1990s allegations of child abuse by Michael Jackson were among the most well-known controversies surrounding him. A well-publicized trial ensued when a 13-year-old child accused Jackson of sexual molestation in 1993. In the end, the matter was resolved out of court for a sizable sum, but Jackson's image suffered permanent harm.

The publication of the documentary "Living with Michael Jackson" in 2003 sparked yet another major controversy. In the documentary, which was produced by Martin Bashir, Jackson was seen holding hands with a little child and talking about his unusual lifestyle, which painted him in an unflattering light. This stoked rumors about Jackson's contacts with kids and raised questions about how suitable his interactions were.

Additionally, Jackson's supposed physical metamorphosis came under heavy public attention. The singer's evolving look over time, which has been linked to many cosmetic procedures, has generated a lot of conversation about body dysmorphia and the demands of celebrity. These alterations were often sensationalized by the media, which fueled conjecture and theories about Jackson's self-perception.

Another area of Jackson's life that sparked media curiosity was his financial difficulties. Despite his enormous success, he struggled financially and had to sell off priceless possessions to pay off debt, including the Beatles library. Jackson's financial difficulties were extensively covered by the media, which furthered the public's negative opinion of him.

The pop star's marriages to Lisa Marie Presley and Debbie Rowe, among other partnerships, were closely followed by the media. Beyond his music, Jackson became well-known due to his high-profile partnerships, as the media scrutinized his personal life dynamics and questioned the sincerity of these partnerships.

Michael Jackson's legacy is still clouded by controversy after his death. When the documentary "Leaving Neverland" was released in 2019, his posthumous reputation was once again called into question. In-depth claims of sexual assault made by two people who said they were Jackson's victims as children were included in the documentary. Jackson's contributions to music were reassessed as a result of the film, which sparked discussions regarding the appropriateness of separating an artist's personal life from their work.

A thorough analysis of both the real Michael Jackson and the fiction is necessary to navigate the media frenzy around him. Though his influence on the music business is indisputable, his reputation has been permanently tarnished by the rumors and scandals that surrounded him. The continuous argument over whether or not to exonerate the artist from the charges highlights how complicated Jackson's story is and raises questions about celebrity, morality, and how the media shapes public opinion.

Michael Jackson published a double album titled HIStory: Past, Present and Future, in 1995. It is a record of his resilience and artistic expression. It was a turning point in his career, presenting a mix of brand-new songs and a list of his best-ever singles. The album is split into two sections: "History Continues" has all new music, and "History Begins" has his biggest hits.

With hits like "Billie Jean," "Beat It," and "Thriller," History Begins serves as a reminder of Michael Jackson's unmatched popularity and influence on the music business. But the section titled HiStory Continues is particularly noteworthy as evidence of Jackson's tenacity and creative expression.

"Scream/Childhood," the album's debut single, is a special mashup of two diametrically opposed songs. "Scream" is a powerful statement of annoyance and fury that addresses both personal hardships and public attention. On the other hand, "Childhood" highlights Jackson's wish to preserve his innocence by reflecting on his own experiences of growing up in the limelight.

"They Don't Care About Us," a song that addresses social concerns and injustice, is also noteworthy. Its strong rhythm and audacious, unvarnished lyrics make it a forceful message against unfairness and prejudice. Jackson was the target of criticism for what some saw to be anti-Semitic lyrics in the first version, which prompted changes in later editions.

The moving song "Stranger in Moscow" explores Jackson's sense of loneliness and isolation. His ability to evoke strong feelings via music is evident in the song's eerie melody and reflective lyrics.

Along with these collaborations, the album includes songs by Boyz II Men and Janet Jackson, including "Scream/Childhood" and "History." These collaborations demonstrate Jackson's impact on and assimilation into a wide range of musical genres.

History encountered difficulties while receiving high praise from critics, including public attention and private conflicts. But the album's lasting significance comes from its ability to convey Jackson's fortitude and creative development. It's an expression of his will to use music to tackle both social concerns and personal challenges, showing off a versatile musician not averse to venturing into uncharted musical territory.

Michael Jackson's HIStory: Past, Present, and Future, Book continues to be a crucial period in his career. It is evidence of his lasting influence on the music business, his fortitude in the face of difficulty, and his dedication to using his work as a vehicle for social criticism and self-expression.

Of course! Let's examine some of the HIStory album's standout tunes and features in more detail:

1."Earth Song": One of *HIStory's best song is this stirring hymn for the earth. The song's symphonic composition and poignant lyrics highlight Jackson's dedication to tackling world challenges. His enthusiasm for environmental activism is further highlighted in the accompanying music video, which has amazing graphics and stirring imagery.

2. "You Are Not Alone": Jackson's tender song, which shot to the top of the charts, "You Are Not Alone" reveals her depth and tenderness. Listeners are moved by the song's personal lyrics and heartfelt delivery, which show a more vulnerable side of the performer.

3. "Tabloid Junkie": In "Tabloid Junkie," Jackson takes aim at the media's invasive reporting of his life. The song's harsh tone and incisive lyrics expose the difficulties he endured as a worldwide celebrity by criticizing the sensationalism and violation of privacy he encountered.

4. Album Concept: HIStory is a conceptual journey through Michael Jackson's life rather than just a compilation of songs. Jackson's historical stature on the record cover represents his influence on the history of music. The listening experience is made more complex by this thematic coherence.

5. Innovative Production: The record combines a variety of musical genres, including pop, rock, R&B, and classical components. The creative production, which is often distinguished by complex layering and experimentation, enhances Jackson's standing as a forward-thinking musician prepared to push the limits of popular music.

6. <u>Commercial Success and Awards:</u> HIStory has several chart-topping hits and had considerable commercial success. It was nominated for several accolades and won several, including a Grammy for Best Music Video for the song "Scream". The album's enduring influence on the music industry is further evidenced by its continued popularity.

7. <u>History World Tour:</u> Jackson started one of the most popular concert tours in history, the HIStory World Tour, to promote the album. The tour confirmed his reputation as an incredible live performer by showcasing his unmatched stage presence and lavish sets.

8. <u>History's Legacy and Ongoing Influence:</u> History is still hailed as a key album in Michael Jackson's discography. Its themes of tenacity, social criticism, and creative exploration have impacted artists in later generations, cementing Jackson's reputation as the "King of Pop."

HIStory is essentially a multimedia examination of Michael Jackson's life, hardships, and artistic abilities rather than merely an album. Its enduring influence stems from both its hit songs that reached the top of the charts and its ability to depict the intricacies of an iconic artist juggling fame, personal struggles, and a changing world.

The Return of the King: This and Beyond

"The King's Comeback: This Is It and Beyond" highlights a pivotal time in the life and career of Michael Jackson, the pop icon. "This Is It," the highly anticipated concert series that was scheduled to take place in 2009 at London's O2 Arena, served as the centerpiece of this comeback. Unfortunately, Michael Jackson died on June 25, 2009, only weeks before the planned appearances.

Following a significant break from live performances, Jackson was scheduled to make his stage comeback with the "This Is It" concerts. The news of the tour caused fans all over the world to become extremely excited. The King of Pop has fifty shows scheduled to include his legendary tunes from his long and successful career. The purpose of these performers was to honor Michael Jackson's legacy and demonstrate his continuing influence on the music business.

The planning for the concerts provides an insight into the rigorous and imaginative approach Jackson took to his performances. Renowned choreographers, stage designers, and musicians united to produce a magnificent spectacle. The rehearsals, shown in the film "This Is It," demonstrated Jackson's attention to excellence and his desire to produce an unequaled live experience.

After Jackson's unexpected death, the "This Is It" film was released, affording fans a sad behind-the-scenes look at the planning for the performances. The documentary revealed Jackson's creative process, the intricate stage settings, and the extraordinary skill that marked his performances. The film became a posthumous homage to the artist and presented admirers with a melancholy insight into what may have been.

Beyond the "This Is It" period, Michael Jackson's impact lives via his iconic songs and innovative contributions to the entertainment business. His influence extends to future generations of artists, and his imprint on pop culture remains incalculable. The King's return may have been brutally cut short, but his creative stamp continues to resound, guaranteeing that Michael Jackson remains an enduring legend in the field of music and performance.

The King's Comeback stretched beyond the "This Is It" performances, as Michael Jackson's influence continued to alter the music business posthumously. Following his demise, there was a rise in interest and admiration for his huge record of hits. Fans rediscovered favorites like "Thriller," "Billie Jean," and "Smooth Criminal," catapulting these songs back into the charts and exposing a new generation to Jackson's unrivaled craftsmanship.

In addition, Michael Jackson's influence was seen in the dance and fashion industries. His distinctive looks—which included the recognizable fedora, gloves, and coats with military accents—became timeless icons of popular culture. He made the moonwalk a famous dance technique that was often imitated by performers paying respect to the King of Pop. It became a mainstay in dance routines.

Michael Jackson's legacy in the music industry was further cemented in the years that followed his death with posthumous albums. Records such as "Xscape" included previously unheard tracks and reworked versions of his hits, demonstrating the breadth of his back catalog and the enduring value of his compositions.

The good effects of Michael Jackson's charitable endeavors extended beyond the music industry. His altruistic donations to organizations supporting HIV/AIDS research, children's hospitals, and disaster assistance have created a long-lasting humanitarian impact. Cirque du Soleil's Michael Jackson ONE performance in Las Vegas is a lasting tribute to the pop icon, providing viewers with an unforgettable and visually spectacular experience.

The expectation of never-to-be-held live concerts may have accompanied the King's Comeback, but Michael Jackson's legacy endures thanks to the persistent popularity of his songs, their continuing effect on modern musicians, and their lasting impression on popular culture. The King of Pop's journey goes beyond his physical presence on Earth, serving as a constant reminder that his influence will be felt for many years to come.

CHAPTER 6

Legacy of the Gloved One

<u>Immortalized music: posthumous releases and tributes</u>

With his exceptional skill and iconic contributions, Michael Jackson, often called the "King of Pop", left a lasting impact on the music industry. Even after his untimely death at the age of 50 on June 25, 2009, his legacy continued through posthumous releases and tributes that aimed to immortalize his impact on the music world.

The release of the album "Michael" in December 2010 was one of the most important releases after his death. The album, which included songs Jackson had recorded before his death, generated excitement and controversy. Fans and critics argued about Jackson's vocals' authenticity on some songs, leading to discussions about the morality of releasing unfinished work. After the controversy, "Michael" included collaborations with famous artists such as Akon, 50 Cent and Lenny Kravitz, highlighting Jackson's lasting influence.

The compilation album "Xscape", released in 2014, was another notable project after his passing. The album, which was executive produced by LA Reid, featured previously unreleased recordings from Jackson's collection, which were reworked and modernized by contemporary producers such as Timbaland and Rodney Jerkins. "Xscape" received praise for its respect for Jackson's heritage, and the revamped tracks offered a new perspective on the artist's creative process.

In addition to the posthumous albums, several tribute events honored Michael Jackson's musical journey. In honor of the late pop icon, "Michael Forever: The Tribute Concert" took place in October 2011 at the Millennium Stadium in Cardiff, Wales, featuring a lineup of notable artists including Beyoncé, Christina Aguilera and Smokey Robinson. Although the concert received criticism for the absence of Jackson's close family and some fans expressed concern about the commercial nature of the event, it served as a platform for artists to pay tribute to the King of Pop.

The stage production "Michael Jackson: The Immortal World Tour" was also created, which premiered in 2011. Acrobatics, dance, and visual effects were combined with Jackson's timeless music to create a unique and immersive experience for viewers around the world. The success of the tour emphasized the enduring popularity of Michael Jackson's catalog and showed how his artistry could be reinvented for new generations.

There is no doubt that Michael Jackson's impact on the music industry goes beyond his physical presence. The constant admiration and respect for the King of Pop is reflected in the continued efforts to honor and remember his contributions through albums, tributes and live performances, ensuring that his music remains an immortal treasure for many years to come.

Pop Culture Impact: Michael Jackson's Lasting Influence

Michael Jackson's lasting impact on pop culture is undoubted, as he left a lasting impact on the music and entertainment industry. Jackson's impact goes beyond his extraordinary musical talent, although he is often called the "King of Pop." Many facets of popular culture can be influenced by it, such as music, dance, fashion, and even how celebrities interact with their audiences.

- ❖ Musical heritage:

Michael Jackson's contribution to music transformed the industry. The album "Thriller", which came out in 1982, remains the best-selling album of all time. The iconic title track, along with hits like "Billie Jean" and "Beat It," not only dominated the charts, but also set new standards for pop and R&B music. As seen in the groundbreaking "Thriller" video, his inventive use of music videos transformed the medium into an art form and became a cultural phenomenon.

❖ Immortalized music: posthumous releases and tributes

With his exceptional skill and iconic contributions, Michael Jackson, often called the "King of Pop", left a lasting impact on the music industry. Even after his untimely death at the age of 50 on June 25, 2009, his legacy continued through posthumous releases and tributes that aimed to immortalize his impact on the world of music.

The release of the album "Michael" in December 2010 was one of the biggest releases after his death. The album, which included songs Jackson had recorded before his death, generated excitement and controversy. Fans and critics argued over the authenticity of Jackson's voice on some songs, leading to discussions about the morality of releasing unfinished works. After the controversy, "Michael" included collaborations with famous artists such as Akon, 50 Cent and Lenny Kravitz, highlighting Jackson's lasting influence.

The compilation album "Xscape," released in 2014, was another notable project following his passing. The album, which was produced by LA Reid, featured previously unreleased recordings from Jackson's collection, which were reworked and modernized by contemporary producers such as Timbaland and Rodney Jerkins. "Xscape" received praise for ts respect for Jackson's heritage and the revamped tracks offered new insight into the artist's creative process.

In addition to the posthumous albums, several tribute events honored Michael Jackson's musical journey. In honor of the late pop icon, "Michael Forever: The Tribute Concert" took place in October 2011 at the Millennium Stadium in Cardiff, Wales, with a lineup of notable artists including Beyoncé, Christina Aguilera and Smokey Robinson. Although the concert received criticism for the absence of Jackson's close family members and some fans expressed concern about the commercial nature of the event, it served as a platform for artists to pay tribute to the King of Pop.

The stage production "Michael Jackson: The Immortal World Tour" was also created, premiering in 2011. Stunts, dance, and visual effects were combined with Jackson's timeless music to create a unique and immersive experience for moviegoers. everyone. The success of the tour emphasized the enduring popularity of Michael Jackson's catalog and showed how his artistry could be reinvented for new generations.

There is no doubt that Michael Jackson's impact on the music industry goes beyond his physical presence. The constant admiration and respect for the King of Pop is reflected in the continued efforts to honor and remember his contributions through albums, tributes and live performances, ensuring that his music remains an immortal treasure for many years to come. come. .

Pop Culture Impact: The Lasting Influence of Michael Jackson

Michael Jackson's lasting impact on pop culture is undoubted, as he left a lasting impact on the music and entertainment industry. Jackson's impact goes beyond his extraordinary musical talent, although he is often called the "King of Pop." Many facets of popular culture can be influenced by it, such as music, dance, fashion, and even the way celebrities interact with its audience.

- ❖ Musical heritage:

Michael Jackson's contribution to music transformed the industry. The album "Thriller", released in 1982, remains the best-selling album of all time. The iconic title track, along with hits like "Billie Jean" and "Beat It," not only dominated the charts, but also set new standards for pop and R&B music. As seen in the groundbreaking "Thriller" video, his inventive use of music videos transformed the medium into an art form and became a cultural phenomenon.

CHAPTER 7

Behind the Mask

<u>Individual Battles: The Demons Michael Met with</u>

Michael Jackson, a.k.a. the "King of Pop," was a legendary musician renowned for his tremendous skill and widespread influence. But in the background, he dealt with a host of personal issues that are comparable to facing inner demons.

Michael Jackson had many difficulties in life, but his early connection with fame was one of the biggest. At the age of six, he began performing with the Jackson 5, and he quickly rose to fame all over the world. He struggled greatly with his identity as a result of the strain and attention that came with his achievement. His public image and his inner nature were in continual conflict because of the demands put on him as a performer and public figure.

Michael also had physical health problems that had a big influence on his life. His skin tone changed as a result of his vitiligo, which sparked rumors and condemnation from the public. This increased the pressure on him to keep up a certain public image. In addition, reports about his many cosmetic surgeries spread, which made his issues with self-image much worse.

A slew of court disputes and scandals also characterized the singer's private life. The accusations of child molestation he was the subject of in the early 1990s were one of the most prominent. Even though he was found not guilty in a well reported trial, the allegations negatively impacted his mental and emotional health and permanently changed the way the public saw him.

Jackson's financial troubles also plagued him. Even with his great accomplishments, he was in a hazardous financial condition due to careless money management and wasteful spending. This added to the weight of his personal troubles by resulting in court fights and, eventually, the selling of his precious music archive.

The dynamics between Michael Jackson and his family were very complicated. Concerns over the influence of his early years on his adult life were raised by reports of a tense relationship between him and his father, Joe Jackson. His marriages and divorces also emphasized the difficulties he had in preserving interpersonal relationships in the face of his international celebrity.

Michael found comfort in his art and charity throughout his life. He expressed his emotions via music, and his humanitarian endeavors, such as supporting different organizations, demonstrated his desire to have a good influence on the world.

Michael Jackson ultimately faced several challenges in his personal life, including problems with his identity, health, legal troubles, money problems, and complicated relationships. Notwithstanding these obstacles, he continues to have a profound effect on the music business, and his creative legacy is still influencing fans and artists throughout the globe.

The difficulties Michael Jackson faced went beyond his private life and notoriety. His mental health suffered as a result of the sensationalized reports and ongoing media attention. He was often the target of controversy, having to deal with harsh criticism and tabloid rumors. This constant exposure to the spotlight produced a solitary atmosphere that exacerbated emotions of alienation and loneliness.

The pop icon's personal issues were partly a result of his dedication to job excellence. He was under a lot of pressure to maintain his high standards since he was well-known for paying close attention to detail in both his music and performances. Perfectionism helped him become a brilliant artist, but it also caused great stress and difficult-to-maintain demands for himself.

In addition, Michael's changing look ignited a deeper story of self-acceptance in addition to rumors. The debate over his evolving physical appearance provided insight into the influence that society's standards of beauty had on his self-worth. This battle with his body image and the pressures of society fed his inner demons even more.

An additional facet of the singer's personal challenges was his spiritual journey. Michael, who was raised as a Jehovah's Witness, had difficulties balancing his religious convictions with his widespread celebrity and the sometimes hedonistic entertainment business. The internal struggle he had throughout his life gave the demons he battled a spiritual aspect.

Michael Jackson overcame these obstacles, and his perseverance was evident in his work. He channeled his feelings into classic songs that millions of others could relate to via his creative outlet as a coping strategy. His desire to promote good change in the world and address some of the difficulties he personally experienced and saw throughout the globe is reflected in songs like "Man in the Mirror" and "Heal the World".

Michael Jackson's legacy lives on not only because of his musical accomplishments but also because of his bravery in facing his inner demons via his work when faced with hardship. His life is a complicated story filled with victories and setbacks that have a long-lasting effect on the music business as well as on culture at large.

The Mysterious Persona: Revealing the Individual Hidden Behind the Mask

The "King of Pop," was a versatile performer who had unmatched success in the music business. Michael Joseph Jackson, born in Gary, Indiana, on August 29, 1958, started his career early as a member of the Jackson 5, a Motown group he created with his siblings. However, it was his solo endeavors that shot him to international fame and left a lasting impression on the entertainment industry.

Michael Jackson's secretive identity is defined by a number of elements, such as his dancing, music, dress, and the cryptic atmosphere that surrounds him all of his life. A very recognizable feature of his character was his continuous development, both in terms of music and appearance. From the Motown heyday to the revolutionary "Thriller" period, Michael Jackson continuously explored creative frontiers, evolving with every record.

Jackson's songs cut across genres and age groups because of their catchy rhythms and avant-garde vibe. 1982 saw the release of his record "Thriller," which is still the best-selling album ever. The John Landis-directed music video for the title tune, which showcased Michael Jackson's signature dancing movements and innovative use of special effects, went viral.

The enigma surrounding Michael Jackson is partly a result of his constantly shifting physical attributes. Jackson's look changed dramatically throughout the years, leading to rumors regarding skin disorders and cosmetic surgery. His shifting skin tone came under considerable public observation, which sparked debates and suspicions.

Beyond his musical abilities, Jackson's generosity and humanitarian work revealed another aspect of his mysterious character. He was a supporter of several humanitarian initiatives, such as organizations that fight sickness, disaster assistance, and children's hospitals.

But when Jackson dealt with legal issues, the mystery became more complex. He was charged with child molestation in 1993; the matter was settled out of court. In a more well-known trial in 2005, Jackson was found not guilty of any of the charges. His public image became more complicated as a result of these court disputes, raising numerous unresolved concerns.

Jackson's peculiar actions and peculiarities in his personal life added to the mystique around him. The building of his huge ranch, Neverland Ranch, which had a movie theater, zoo, and amusement park, increased the mystery. Jackson's love of animals and his innocent demeanor encouraged rumors about his unconventional lifestyle and innocence.

Michael Jackson tragically went away at the age of 50 on June 25, 2009, marking the tragic end of his life. His death's circumstances—which were determined to be acute propofol and benzodiazepine intoxication—sparked many debates and inquiries.

It becomes evident that Michael Jackson's life was a rich tapestry of contrasts when the man behind the mask is revealed. Even while he has had a lasting impression on the music business, both fans and critics are still enthralled and perplexed by the mysterious character he has developed over the years.

Beyond his career and personal life, Michael Jackson cultivated an intriguing image that delved into imagination and mysticism. His love of the paranormal and otherworldly is apparent in his stage plays, music videos, and even the name of his house, Neverland Ranch, which is a reference to J.M. Barrie's made-up world from "Peter Pan."

Jackson's reputation as a visionary was further cemented by his partnerships with well-known filmmakers and artists. His creative use of special effects and the recognizable anti-gravity lean were on display in the short video for "Smooth Criminal," which was included in the "Moonwalker" anthology. His dedication to pushing technological limits in music videos became a signature move for his business.

The music icon's mystery was further compounded by his interactions with the media and celebrity. Although he often voiced unease about the intrusive aspect of the spotlight, his lavish theatrical productions and well-produced music videos were meant for a wide audience. The enigma surrounding his actual identity was heightened by this contradictory connection with celebrity.

Another aspect of Jackson's legacy is his effect on dancing. He made the moonwalk famous, and it has since been associated with his name and is now one of the most recognizable dancing moves ever. His remarkable theatrical presence and elaborate choreography made him a worldwide cultural phenomenon.

Moreover, it is impossible to overestimate Michael Jackson's influence on racial and cultural boundaries. As an African American musician, he dismantled racial boundaries in the music business, succeeding in crossover and winning over a broad range of fans. His philanthropic endeavors also demonstrated his dedication to advancing harmony and understanding.

Jackson's financial circumstances added to the mystery around him. Even though he had great economic success, there were rumors of financial difficulties and legal disputes around his inheritance. His legacy became more complicated once the Beatles' catalog rights were sold to Sony in the 1980s and after more financial transactions.

When trying to find out who is behind Michael Jackson's mask, one comes up with a person who is difficult to define.

Contradictions, disputes, and a never-ending pursuit of creative originality characterized his life. Long after his death, Michael Jackson remains a fascinating and intriguing figure due to the mystery that surrounds him.

Ties between family, friends, and confidantes in Neverland

"Relationships in Neverland: Family, Friends, and Confidantes of Michael Jackson"

Jackson maintained a complicated network of ties at his exclusive retreat, Neverland Ranch. The connections in Neverland, from friendships to family ties to confidantes in high regard, were vital in molding the life of this legendary singer.

❖ Relationships with Family:

In addition to being a fantastical estate, Michael treasured the family memories he had in Neverland.

His father created an enchanted environment that his three children, Prince, Paris, and Blanket, often spent time in. Even with all of the controversy surrounding his personal life, Michael's children remained the center of his universe. Their longing for normality in the middle of their father's remarkable existence was evident in their presence at Neverland.

❖ Near Friends:

Friendships with Michael Jackson went beyond the showbiz aspect of the music business. The renowned actress Elizabeth Taylor was one of his closest pals. Their relationship was

90

beyond the ordinary friendship between two celebrities; Taylor was even appointed as Michael's children's godmother. Macaulay Culkin, the kid star of "Home Alone," was another well-known buddy. He spent a lot of time in Neverland and even testified in court on Michael's behalf.

❖ Partners and Confidantes:

Michael worked creatively with some of the biggest names in the music business while residing in Neverland. Jackson's career was significantly shaped by famed producer Quincy Jones, who worked with him to create some of his most well-known records. Beyond only working together professionally, Jackson and Jones had a friendship based on respect for one another and a common goal of creating innovative music.

Apart from his colleagues in the workplace, Michael had close friends who offered emotional support. One such person who had a close relationship with Jackson was the spiritual teacher and author Deepak Chopra. Their bond extended into spiritual realms, providing Michael with comfort in trying times.

- ❖ Difficulties and Debates:

Neverland served as Michael's haven, but it also turned into a hotbed of controversy. When accusations of child abuse emerged, court fights ensued, casting a shadow on his relationships. The claims revealed the weakness within Neverland's closed doors and caused tension with certain friends and family members.

- ❖ Afterglow of Neverland Connections:

Michael Jackson's legacy includes the connections he established in Neverland. The close relationships he had with friends, family, and confidantes show the human aspect of a worldwide cultural phenomenon, despite the criticisms and difficulties. The enchanted atmosphere of Neverland provided a setting for these connections, irrevocably altering the course of Michael Jackson's life and career.

CHAPTER 8

Michael's Business

<u>The Jackson Empire: Music and Memorabilia</u>

The Jackson Empire is a symbol of a complex legacy that transcends music and encompasses a sizable empire of goods and cultural impact. The Jackson family, especially the illustrious Michael Jackson and his siblings, is the center of this enterprise.

❖ Basis for Music:

The Jacksons—the siblings Jackie, Tito, Jermaine, Marlon, and a young Michael—became well-known in the music business as The Jackson 5 in the late 1960s. "I Want You Back" and "ABC," two of their Motown singles, catapulted them to global fame. Particularly during his solo career, Michael Jackson became a worldwide phenomenon with albums such as "Off the Wall," "Thriller," and "Bad."

- ❖ Pop Culture Influence:

The Jacksons have had an enormous influence on popular culture. Michael Jackson's trademark fedora, glove, and moonwalk all come to represent his artistic abilities. The 1982 album Thriller is still the record that has sold the most copies worldwide. The music videos, particularly "Thriller," transformed the format and raised the bar for artistic excellence.

- ❖ The Success of Merchandising:

The Jacksons entered the merchandise business as their fame grew. Selling Michael Jackson memorabilia, such as apparel, posters, and collectibles, turned into a profitable part of their business. The continuing demand for Michael Jackson's products may be attributed to the famous iconography connected with his different periods.

- ❖ MJ's Worldwide Identity:

Beyond only music, Michael Jackson himself became a brand. His image and brand partnerships spread across a variety of industries, such as video games, fashion, and fragrances. MJ's influence may be seen in his endorsement agreements with well-known companies and in his founding of businesses like the entertainment firm MJJ Productions.

- ❖ Beyond Neverland Ranch:

Michael Jackson's aim to create a fanciful world of entertainment and pleasure was shown by his investment in Neverland Ranch. There was a theater, a zoo, and an amusement park on the grounds. Even though the ranch was financially unstable, it represented Jackson's desire to expand his brand into other lifestyle endeavors.

- ❖ Remembrances After Death:

The Jackson Empire grew even after Michael Jackson's tragic passing in 2009. The legacy was preserved via posthumous record releases, hologram shows, and partnerships with modern musicians. "Michael Jackson: The Immortal World Tour," a Cirque du Soleil production, strengthened Jackson's lasting influence even further.

- ❖ Legal Conflicts and Obstacles:

Legal disputes about Michael Jackson's estate have been among the many difficulties the Jackson family has had to deal with. The family's undertakings have become more complicated as a result of inheritance disputes and allegations made against those in charge of the estate administration.

The Jackson Empire is proof of the long-lasting legacy of a family that not only influenced music but also expertly handled the complex worlds of commerce and cultural impact. With Michael Jackson as its brightest star, the Jacksons' legacy lives on via music, clothing, and other cultural endeavors, creating a lasting impression on future generations.

❖ Humanitarian and Philanthropic Activities:

The Jackson family has been heavily interested in charity in addition to music and products. Particularly well-known for his philanthropic support of several causes, such as HIV/AIDS research, children's hospitals, and disaster relief, was Michael Jackson. His commitment to social justice gave the Jackson Empire a more humane aspect.

❖ Ventures in Multimedia:

The Jacksons moved into multimedia companies in addition to music. This covers Michael Jackson's entry into the movie industry with the ground-breaking "Thriller" music video and his roles in movies such as "Moonwalker." The family's varied portfolio was further enhanced by their exploration of multimedia initiatives such as television production.

❖ Innovating in Art:

Creative innovation is influenced by the Jackson Empire. Known as the "King of Pop," Michael Jackson was a continual innovator in dance, music, and visual storytelling. His avant-garde music videos and ground-breaking live performances revolutionized the entertainment industry by raising the bar for originality and inventiveness.

❖ Style and Fashion Icon:

The Jacksons, particularly Michael, have had a lasting impression on the world of fashion. Michael established an iconic look with his use of sequined gloves, fedoras, and military coats. The popularization of styles that went beyond music is another way in which the family's influence on fashion has contributed significantly to their cultural effect.

❖ Worldwide Fan Base:

The Jacksons' devoted following is evidence of their ongoing appeal. The "Moonwalkers," a worldwide fan community, are still honored for the family's contributions to music and culture. The Jackson Empire remains vibrant because of fan activities, tribute performances, and social media interaction.

- Learning Projects:

The Jacksons have supported talent development and arts education via their involvement in educational programs. Michael Jackson's support of educational institutions and arts-oriented initiatives is indicative of his commitment to nurturing artistic abilities and creativity. These programs add to the family's history of supporting creative education.

- Estate Planning and Legacy Management:

Careful estate planning is necessary to manage a worldwide superstar like Michael Jackson's legacy. The Jackson Empire has successfully handled obstacles pertaining to copyright, intellectual property, and maintaining Michael Jackson's creative integrity. The family heritage will continue to expand and be preserved thanks to the estate's diligent administration.

- Perseverance in Culture:

The Jackson Empire continues to be referenced in current art, fashion, and music, demonstrating its continuing cultural legacy. The Jacksons' cultural longevity is proof of the everlasting value of their contributions to the entertainment business, from award show tributes to reimaginings of their famous music videos.

Beyond the worlds of music and merchandising, the Jackson Empire leaves behind a rich legacy. The Jackson family has had an enduring and worldwide effect on the entertainment industry via charity, multimedia endeavors, creative innovation, and lasting cultural influence.

Conflicts over contracts, copyrights, and other legal issues

The King of Pop, Michael Jackson, was well-known for the legal disputes and scandals that dogged his career in addition to his immeasurable contributions to the music business. A prominent legal challenge he encountered concerned copyrights.

Jackson's acquisition of the songwriting rights to several Beatles compositions in the 1980s led to a legal dispute with founding member Paul McCartney. The connection between Jackson and McCartney was damaged by the purchase of the ATV music collection, which included successes by the

Beatles. Over time, Jackson's calculated investment paid off despite the uproar.

When Jackson's album "Dangerous" was released in 1991, a major new copyright dispute arose. Belgian artist Jacques Loussier accused the title track of violating his copyright since it was similar to his song "Pulsion." The case brought to light the difficulties faced by artists in walking the thin line between inspiration and infringement, even if it was resolved out of court.

Jackson's legal background also included contractual conflicts. The dispute with Sony Music was one of the most well-known incidents. Early in the new millennium, Michael Jackson said that Sony was mismanaging the release of his album "Invincible" and that the company had excessive influence over his career. Jackson and the music mogul had a tense relationship as a result, with the performer openly criticizing the industry's predatory methods.

When Michael Jackson went through a well reported trial in 2005 on allegations of child abuse, the debate surrounding him reached a turning point. After a protracted trial that lasted many months, Jackson was found not guilty of any of the charges. However, the trial left a lasting impression on the public and added to the continuing discussions about his private life.

Michael Jackson continues to have an unmatched influence on the music business in spite of the legal issues. His influence on pop culture and the controversy that surrounded his career have had a lasting impression on the entertainment industry. The legal disputes involving contracts, copyrights, and other issues highlight how complicated the music business is and how difficult it is for well-known performers like Michael Jackson.

Michael's Excursions Outside the Theater

Michael Jackson showed his versatility with a variety of off-stage endeavors. In addition to becoming the "King of

Pop," Michael Jackson was an astute businessman, humanitarian, and performer.

- ❖ Rights to Music Publication:

The Beatles' songs were among the many tunes that Jackson acquired the music publishing rights to, making it one of his biggest financial decisions. He outbid rivals to acquire ATV Music Publishing, which owned the rights to several well-known songs, in the 1980s. This astute investment not only brought him a sizable salary but also cemented his power in the music business.

- ❖ Career in Film:

Even though he is most recognized for his singing, Michael Jackson dabbled in the movie business. Alongside Diana Ross, he appeared in the musical adaption of "The Wizard of Oz," "The Wiz" (1978). His cinematic career proved his flexibility as a performer, even if it didn't reach the same heights as his musical accomplishments.

- ❖ Entrepreneurship:

Jackson dabbled in a number of business ventures, starting MJJ Productions, his own entertainment firm. This production business worked on movies, video games, and even music. He was able to sustain financial success outside of his singing career by diversifying his sources of income and using his business expertise.

❖ Charitable Giving:

Michael Jackson pursued philanthropic endeavors vigorously. Notably, he and Lionel Richie co-wrote the charity record "We Are the World". Jackson's dedication to utilizing his fame for good in society is evident in the song's revenues, which were donated to aid those affected by the famine in Africa. He was an advocate for a number of charity causes, especially those that touched on the health and education of children.

❖ Advertising and Sponsorships:

Because of his reputation and appeal, Jackson was able to sign lucrative endorsement and merchandising contracts. His image appeared on a number of items, and he entered into profitable collaborations, which enhanced his total wealth.

❖ Investment in Theme Parks:

Michael Jackson contributed to the "Captain EO" 3D movie's production for Disney theme parks in the late 1980s. His nterest in cutting-edge entertainment endeavors outside of the conventional music business was further shown by this effort.

Michael Jackson's activities beyond the stage demonstrated his brilliance and importance not just as a singer but also as a multidimensional and prominent personality in different sectors, despite encountering financial troubles later in life, including legal issues and debts.

CHAPTER 9

Symphony of Images

Making Iconic Music Videos: A Creative Adventure
"Creating Iconic Music Videos: An Artistic Journey of Michael Jackson"

Michael Jackson, who is sometimes referred to as the "King of Pop," not only transformed the music business with his ground-breaking albums but also permanently altered the visual narrative landscape with his legendary music videos. His creative process in making these films is evidence of his inventiveness, originality, and commitment to pushing the envelope in the entertainment industry.

"Thriller," which debuted in 1983, is without a doubt one of the most iconic music videos in history. John Landis directed this 14-minute epic, which combined the force of music and cinematic narrative with Michael Jackson's unmatched dancing skills. The storyline of the video, which showed Jackson changing into a werewolf in the middle of an undead lance, enthralled viewers all over the globe. Theatrical elements, dancing, and state-of-the-art special effects took "Thriller" from a music video to a phenomenon that captivated audiences.

The popularity of "Thriller" inspired Jackson to create a number of breathtakingly beautiful music videos. 1988 saw the release of "Smooth Criminal," another classic. Colin Chilvers directed it, and it showcases Jackson's trademark lean as well as the creative "anti-gravity" maneuver. Jackson's riveting performance is combined with aspects of criminal drama to create a tale that is reminiscent of cinema noir. Its ageless appeal was aided by the utilization of a 1930s look and Michael Jackson's trademark dancing technique.

For the 1995 video of "Scream," a duet with his sister Janet Jackson, Jackson worked with filmmaker Mark Romanek. In addition to being visually arresting, this spaceship-themed future film also served as a warning about the cost of celebrity and media scrutiny. As one of the most costly music videos ever made, "Scream" continues to wow with its slick design and cutting-edge graphics.

With the John Landis-directed "Black or White" (1991) music video, Jackson maintained his dedication to telling a tale via his music videos. In this movie, which included state-of-the-art morphing technology that allowed Jackson to effortlessly shift into numerous people from different ethnic origins, themes of unity and diversity were addressed. The message of the film and its worldwide appeal struck a chord with viewers everywhere.

Jackson's films often tackled societal themes in addition to being visually stunning. Spike Lee's 1996 film "They Don't Care About Us" tackled issues of racial injustice and prejudice. The video, which was shot in Brazilian favelas and included passionate performances by Jackson, made a strong message about human rights.

The creative process that Michael Jackson went through to create his music videos is evidence of his ability to combine narrative with music to create a coherent and powerful art form. His music videos not only demonstrated his tremendous skill as a performer, but they also raised the bar for originality and inventiveness in the music business. Every video was a masterfully produced work of art that added to Michael Jackson's overall reputation as a great entertainment pioneer.

The Enchantment of Michael's Dance: Joint Ventures and Novelties

"The Magic of Michael's Choreography: Collaborations and Innovations of Michael Jackson"

The King of Pop, Michael Jackson, not only transformed the music business with his ground-breaking records but also permanently altered the dance world with his unforgettable choreography. In the entertainment sector, his ability to combine rhythm, accuracy, and passion in a seamless manner created a new benchmark. Let's investigate Michael's creative contributions and partnerships as we explore the enchantment of his dance.

❖ Joint Ventures:

Michael and Michael Peters' collaboration: Michael Jackson's dancing career included a significant partnership with choreographer Michael Peters. Their partnership produced the enduring dance move for "Beat It." The video's synced and exuberant motions became a signature of Michael's style.

Working together with Jeffrey Daniel: Michael was first exposed to the dance known as the "Backslide," which became known as the moonwalk thanks in large part to Jeffrey Daniel. One of the most recognizable dancing moves in music history, this motion will always be connected to Michael Jackson.

The Bob Fosse Effect: Michael's work demonstrates his respect for the renowned Broadway choreographer Bob Fosse. Fosse's influence is evident in Jackson's deft and elegant movements, which give his performances a sophisticated touch—most especially in "Smooth Criminal."

- ❖ Novelties:

The moonwalk, or a. The moonwalk, perhaps the most well-known dancing technique linked to Michael Jackson, was revolutionary. Its illusory gliding motion came to represent his extraordinary ability and inventiveness as a dancer.

"Smooth Criminal"'s Anti-Gravity Lean: In the "Smooth Criminal" music video, a leaning forward harness and specially made shoes allowed for a gravity-defying lean.

Michael's inventiveness demonstrated his dedication to expanding the realm of performing possibilities.

Including Street Dancing: Michael Jackson was an expert at smoothly combining several dancing forms. His use of popping and locking, two street dance techniques, gave his choreography a modern edge and connected with a wide range of viewers.

❖ Pop Culture Impact:

International Dancing Phenomenon: The choreography of Michael Jackson cut beyond national and cultural barriers. His dance routines became well-known around the globe, and many dancers and artists were influenced to adopt his technique.

Dance Narratives with Music Videos: Michael Jackson transformed music videos into elaborate dance dramas, elevating the notion of music videos. Every video turned into a visual extravaganza with creative choreography that complimented the songs' narrative elements.

Not only does Michael's choreography possess inherent magic, but it also benefits from his partnerships with other visionaries in the dance community. Generations of dancers are still influenced by his ideas, and his effect on pop culture is unmatched. The ageless power of dance as a global language that unites people through rhythm and movement is shown by Michael Jackson's choreography.

The Visual Extravaganza: Musicals, Tours, and Magnificent Exhibitions

Michael Jackson was well-known for his innovative music as well as for his visually stunning tours, concerts, and performances, all of which had a lasting impression on the entertainment business. As one of the most recognizable characters in popular music history, Michael Jackson turned live concerts into works of art by fusing unmatched stage design, inventive technology, and charisma.

The 1987–1989 "Bad World Tour" was one of the high points in Michael Jackson's musical career and it revolutionized live performances. Millions of admirers from all around the globe attended the 16-month tour, which stopped in 15 different countries. A sophisticated lighting system, pyrotechnics, and hydraulic lifts were all part of the enormous stage arrangement, which produced an amazing visual display. Jackson pushed the limits of what was conceivable in live entertainment at the time by interacting with virtual characters via the use of cutting-edge technology, including the first-ever projection system on a concert tour.

With the "Dangerous World Tour" (1992–1993), Jackson further cemented his reputation as a master of visual spectacle. The tour not only showcased Jackson's musical brilliance but also his dedication to pushing the frontiers of stage production, introducing the world to the legendary "Dangerous" record. The performances benefited from the utilization of elaborate set designs, which included a revolving stage and a huge robotic panther. The tour also established a standard for live entertainment in the 1990s with its use of sophisticated choreography and state-of-the-art visual effects.

But the "HIStory World Tour" (1996–1997) was the real pinnacle of Michael Jackson's ability to produce spectacular shows. Supporting the "HIStory: Past, Present and Future, Book I" album, this tour included a massive stage with an enormous LED screen showing images from both historical and modern times. The set selection skillfully included songs from the new album together with beloved favorites, giving the audience a vibrant and intense experience.

Michael Jackson's pursuit of excellence in all facets of the production went beyond his singing throughout his career. His partnerships with forward-thinking directors and choreographers, such as Vincent Paterson and Kenny Ortega, produced innovative images that transcended traditional concert settings. Jackson's focus on innovation and meticulous attention to detail made every performance a multimedia feast rather than just a concert.

The 1993 Super Bowl XXVII halftime concert stands as one of Michael Jackson's most famous performances. Jackson captivated the audience of an estimated 90 million people with a performance that included his trademark dances, flawless choreography, and a standout performance of "Billie Jean." The halftime show established the standard for subsequent Super Bowl performances and became a cultural phenomenon.

Innovative stage designs, creative technological applications, and painstaking attention to detail defined Michael Jackson's concerts, tours, and incredible performances. Jackson left behind a legacy that still has an impact on pop culture today because of his skill at fusing dance, music, and visual effects. His dedication to producing unmatched visual spectacles enhanced the live experience and cemented his place in entertainment history.

CHAPTER 10

Harmony in Chaos

Adapting to Public View: Handling Notoriety and Notoriety

Living in the spotlight: Managing Michael Jackson's notoriety and stardom

Known by many as the "King of Pop," Michael Jackson had a life of unequaled celebrity and notoriety. Jackson, who was born in Gary, Indiana, on August 29, 1958, became well-known when he joined his brothers to create the Motown group The Jackson 5. His remarkable path into superstardom began in the 1970s when he decided to pursue a solo career.

❖ Initial Notoriety:

The albums "Off the Wall" and "Thriller" propelled Jackson to international prominence during his early career, which was characterized by extraordinary success. When Thriller was published in 1982, it went on to become the best-selling album ever, further cementing Michael Jackson's reputation as a global superstar. His inventive approach to music and dancing was seen in the accompanying music videos, particularly the ground-breaking Thriller video, which helped catapult Michael into the public eye even further.

❖ Remarkable Notoriety:

Jackson's public profile increased along with the heights of his career. His peculiarities, unusual wardrobe choices, and physical changes—particularly the discoloration of his skin—became regular subjects of tabloid speculation. Jackson's unique lifestyle and mysterious demeanor contributed to the shaping of his public image in addition to his musical accomplishments.

❖ Legal Concerns and Notoriety:

Jackson's latter years were clouded by accusations and legal issues. He was accused of child molestation in 1993, which sparked a well-publicized court fight that ended in an out-of-court settlement. In 2003, a similar instance surfaced, leading to a trial in which he was found not guilty of any crimes. These events severely damaged Jackson's image, putting him under constant investigation and adding to his notoriety.

- ❖ Money Challenges:

Jackson struggled financially despite his enormous success, which forced him to sell off precious possessions and rack up a large debt. His famous home, Neverland Ranch, came to represent both opulence and financial hardship.

- ❖ Scrutiny by the Media:

Jackson endured unrelenting media attention throughout his life, with stories often focused more on his personal life than his musical accomplishments. The tabloids would never stop talking about his marriages, relationships, and parenting style.

- ❖ Mechanisms of Coping:

The relentless scrutiny of the public had a negative impact on Jackson's mental and emotional health. According to reports, he experienced worry, sleeplessness, and even thought about his own death. Jackson used music as a coping method, as well as philanthropic work and keeping a close-knit group of friends and family.

❖ History:

Michael Jackson has had an indisputable effect on the music business, despite the difficulties and controversy. Beyond his sales records, he has influenced music, dance, and entertainment in ways that have shaped the work of many artists. One complicated part of his legacy is the controversy surrounding his personal life, which has sparked continuous discussions about how to distinguish the artist from the person.

Michael Jackson's public life was a complex journey characterized by unheard-of levels of popularity, court disputes, financial hardships, and constant media attention. Jackson, who had to deal with the highs and lows of fame, had a lasting impression on the music industry and cemented his place in pop cultural history.

Tours That Never End: The Joy and Cost of Traveling Life

Tours Without End: The Pleasure and Difficulty of Life on the Road with Michael Jackson

Michael Jackson, widely known as the King of Pop, was well-known for his massive traveling schedule in addition to his innovative songs and memorable live performances. The idea of the Never-Ending Tours came to define Jackson's career, demonstrating his unmatched passion for his work and his unwavering will to reach out to his fans everywhere with his music.

Throughout his career, Jackson went on a number of global tours, beginning with the "Bad World Tour" in 1987–1989, then the "Dangerous World Tour" in 1992–1993 and the historic "HIStory World Tour" in 1996–1997. These tours were more than simply concerts; they were amazing productions that highlighted Michael Jackson's avant-garde dancing, inventive stage presence, and ground-breaking visual effects.

Not only did Michael Jackson feel the excitement of the Never-Ending Tours, but so did his millions of admirers. With Jackson always pushing the limits of live performance, each tour guaranteed an exceptional and memorable experience. Extensive stage designs, sophisticated wardrobe changes, and, of course, Michael Jackson's trademark dancing routines, which enthralled audiences everywhere, were all features of the tours.

But Jackson was not blind to the cost of life on the road. His physical and mental health suffered as a result of his rigorous schedule, constant travel, and pressure to continue performing at a high level. The media's unceasing scrutiny and the difficulties of being in the limelight complicated an already difficult existence.

Jackson's dedication to his followers and love for his music sustained the Never-Ending Tours in spite of the difficulties. His performances evolved into more than simply musical gatherings; they were cultural phenomena that bonded people beyond the limits of time and space.

Sadly, Jackson's health suffered as a result of the Never-Ending Tours, which added to the mental and physical difficulties he had in his final years. The story of his life and career was certainly shaped by the responsibilities of frequent touring in addition to the trappings of celebrity.

Looking back, the Never-Ending Tours continue to be a symbol of Michael Jackson's unparalleled commitment to his craft and his enduring relationship with his worldwide fan base. The excitement and enhancement produced during those concerts are still treasured by fans worldwide as they recall the King of Pop and the enduring impact he made on the music and entertainment industries, despite the obvious toll of life on the road.

Speaking about Michael Jackson's Never-Ending Tours, we must examine the painstaking preparation and execution that went into these enormous shows. Jackson's devotion to excellence could be heard in the minute aspects of his theatrical productions as much as in his music.

A committed group of choreographers, stage designers, costume designers, and technical specialists worked nonstop during the preparation phase to provide the audience with an amazing, technically perfect, and aesthetically pleasing experience. Modern sound systems, state-of-the-art lighting, and creative stage designs took live performances to a whole new level during the concerts.

Jackson's concerts were renowned for their painstaking attention to choreography. Every dance routine was well practiced to guarantee accuracy and coordination among the artists. Fans who experienced Jackson's famous moonwalk, anti-gravity lean in "Smooth Criminal," and other distinctive maneuvers live will always remember them as memorable moments.

The Never-Ending Tours gave Jackson the chance to try out new sounds and musical genres in addition to serving as a platform for his classics. He would often combine jazz, rock, and classical music components into his concerts, giving his fans a dynamic and varied musical experience.

Jackson also used the tours as a forum to spread cultural and social concerns. During his presentations, he often used compelling storytelling and images to convey themes of world peace, environmental awareness, and racial equality. This gave the performances greater substance and made them become a representation of Jackson's dedication to using his art to change the world rather than merely a means of amusement.

Jackson's tenacity and will were shown by the Never-Ending Tours, in spite of the difficulties, which included conflicts and legal disputes. He became a worldwide phenomenon due to his unwavering level of theatrics and ability to fascinate audiences wherever.

The Never-Ending Tours saw their fair share of highs and lows, just like any extended project. Behind-the-scenes reflection and personal challenges often followed the victories on stage. Jackson's road trip was a complicated interaction between achievement, selflessness, and the never-ending quest for creative greatness.

The Never-Ending Tours by Michael Jackson is a living example of the transformational power of live music and the unwavering spirit of a man whose life's work was to use his great skill to inspire, uplift, and unite people. The fans who had the good fortune to see the enchantment of a Michael Jackson concert will always carry the memory of these tours in their hearts.

The Paparazzi Lens: Michael's Struggle with Invasion of Privacy of Michael Jackson

Michael Jackson, was a worldwide celebrity whose life was always in the spotlight. The iconic singer was photographed and shared widely by the paparazzi, who often blurred the boundaries between personal violation and public curiosity.

Jackson's battle with privacy invasion started early in his career, when he became an overnight sensation thanks to hits like "Thriller" and "Bad." Because of his unusual way of living, striking beauty, and mysterious demeanor, he was often the focus of paparazzi looking for interesting photographs and tales.

One of the most well-known events happened in the 1980s when skin disorders and cosmetic surgery began to alter Michael Jackson's look. Seizing on these shifts, the paparazzi produced dramatic headlines and added fuel to the rumors about the singer's private life. Not only did this intensive scrutiny damage Jackson's self-esteem, but it also gave rise to tabloid stories that eclipsed his musical accomplishments.

When Jackson was accused of child abuse in 1993, intrusive media scrutiny peaked. His privacy was severely violated by the circus-like media coverage surrounding the case. He felt as if he was always being watched since helicopters were hovering over his house and paparazzi were stationed outside to record his every move. Jackson's mental health suffered as a result of the invasion, which led to his retreat from the spotlight.

Even after being found not guilty of any charges in 2005, Jackson had to deal with invasive paparazzi attention. Photographers were determined to capture intimate moments despite his reticent lifestyle and efforts to keep his kids out of the limelight. His family's welfare was impacted by this unrelenting investigation in addition to infringing on his right to privacy.

Jackson passed away tragically in 2009, yet the violation of his privacy continued. Following his death, the paparazzi who were looking to make money out of everything about his life continued to provide problems for his family and estate. Court cases arose about the exploitation of Jackson's legacy and the usage of personal photos.

Michael Jackson's case serves as an example of the negative aspects of celebrity culture, where the unrelenting search for dramatic tales may result in privacy violations that have an impact on a person's mental and emotional health in addition to their personal life. Even for individuals who have achieved previously unheard-of heights of popularity, Jackson's struggle serves as a heartbreaking reminder of the necessity of ethical reporting and the need to maintain the boundaries between public and private life.

CHAPTER 11

Warm Remarks

Michael's Romantic Discography: Love Ballads

Michael Jackson is well-known for his seminal contributions to the music business. Even while his lively, danceable tunes are what made him most famous, his beautiful ballads also left a lasting impression. These love ballads reveal a distinct side of Michael Jackson, emphasizing his depth of feeling and his capacity to express genuine emotions via song.

A notable love song by Michael is "I Just Can't Stop Loving You." Entitled "Bad," the song debuted in 1987 as the main single and includes a duet with Siedah Garrett. Their vocals harmonize well, resulting in a strong and moving song that examines the idea of unending love. It's a timeless classic since the accompanying music video heightens the romantic vibe.

Michael's romantic repertoire also includes the wonderful song "You Are Not Alone." When it was published in 1995, his moving ballad became the first-ever song to debut at the top of the Billboard Hot 100 list. The song, which was co-written by R. Kelly, conveys love's certainty and vulnerability. This is one of Jackson's most poignant love ballads because of the deeply felt lyrics and his heartfelt performance.

Michael's mellow and reflective song "Human Nature," which delves into the complexity of human emotions, was released in 1983. Jackson's smooth voice and the song's ethereal melody add to its enduring appeal. "Human Nature" is proof of Michael's capacity to evoke strong feelings in his music, which cuts across genres and has a profound effect on listeners.

Another love ballad that demonstrates Michael's flexibility is the entrancing "Speechless" from the "Invincible" album (2001). The song stands out in his subsequent repertoire because of its emotional lyrics and delicate acoustic arrangement, which evoke feelings of wonder and respect. "Speechless" shows how Jackson has developed as a musician without sacrificing the emotional nuance that has made him famous.

A discussion of Michael Jackson's romantic career would be incomplete, of course, if "The Lady in My Life" from the seminal album "Thriller" (1982) was not included. This R&B ballad with a slow pace is notable for its personal lyrics and soulful music. Jackson's vocal talent is evident, producing a memorable listening experience that appeals to listeners of all ages.

Michael Jackson's romantic record is a veritable gold mine of poignant ballads that demonstrate his range as a performer. These love ballads, which range from the delicate "I Just Can't Stop Loving You" to the powerful "You Are Not Alone" and the classic "Human Nature," perfectly capture Jackson's ability to emotionally connect with listeners. His romantic repertory is nevertheless proof of his continuing influence in the field of love-themed music.

Michael's Jackson parenthood

Michael Jackson, was a father of three. On February 13, 1997, Michael Joseph Jackson Jr., better known as Prince, was born. On April 3, 1998, Paris-Michael Katherine Jackson, his daughter, was born.

The blanket is another name for Prince Michael Jackson II, the third child, who was born on February 21, 2002. Michael had a reputation for keeping his kids mostly out of the spotlight, particularly in their formative years. He took precautions to keep them out of the media and was the guardian of their privacy. After Michael Jackson passed away in 2009, Katherine Jackson, his mother, was named the three children's legal guardian.

According to reports, Michael Jackson was a loving and dedicated father despite his notoriety and unusual lifestyle. Speaking warmly about their father in several interviews and public appearances, his children did so often. Particularly Paris Jackson, who is seeking a career in acting and modeling, has been increasingly noticeable in the media.

There has been much conjecture and mystery regarding the circumstances of Michael's children's conception and birth. Little information regarding the biological mothers' identities was disclosed by Michael, which fueled persistent rumors and conjecture. Whatever their genetic heritage, he always stressed the profound love and relationship he had with his children.

Even though Michael was a discreet dad, it seemed like he focused on giving his kids a sense of normality and morals despite their unique upbringing. The Jackson children carried on Michael Jackson's name and impact by navigating their pathways in the public light, inheriting their father's legacy.

Given his children's unique circumstances, Michael Jackson tried to provide them with as normal a childhood as possible. This was evident in his attitude to parenthood. He requested that they be homeschooled because he thought it would shield them from the negative aspects of being in the spotlight and provide them with a safe space to concentrate on their education.

Even though Michael was well-known across the world, he took care to make sure his kids could have normal life experiences like going to the movies, amusement parks, and the movies without being overrun by photographers. This commitment to keeping children out of the spotlight reflected his complicated relationship with celebrity, having had unrivaled recognition from an early age.

Michael took an active role in his kids' lives by sharing special occasions, going on field excursions, and going to school functions. His kids often spoke about how loving and caring their father was, and how he had a fun and nurturing side. Michael Jackson tried to provide his kids a solid foundation for their futures with a combination of encouragement and discipline.

Following Michael's death in 2009, the three siblings had to make some difficult changes. In particular, Paris Jackson has grown more outspoken about her experiences, pushing for greater public awareness of mental health issues and sharing personal accounts of her challenges. The Jackson kids are carving out unique careers for themselves in a variety of artistic and charitable pursuits, all while upholding their father's legacy.

It's crucial to remember that Michael Jackson's parenting style is still a little mysterious because of his desire to keep his kids out of the limelight. Even if not every detail of their family life has been seen by the public, Michael's dedication as a parent is shown by his concern for his kids' privacy and well-being.

Emotional Lyrics: Interpreting Michael Jackson's Songs' Poetry

Beyond his incredible dance routines and catchy tunes, Michael Jackson's musical legacy includes a great depth of emotional expression that is encapsulated in his words. Jackson was well-known for his ability to blend universal ideas and personal experiences into his songs, and his poetry often went beyond the parameters of conventional pop music.

Michael's emotional depth is most famously seen in "Man in the Mirror." This song, which was released in 1988, is a powerful call for introspection and societal reform. The song's lyrics exhort listeners to examine their own lives and how they could positively influence the world. Unlike many of his previous songs, this contemplative topic showed a more mature and socially conscious side of the performer.

In "Billie Jean," Michael tells a story of love, treachery, and the price of stardom. The lyrics explore the darker side of relationships and the costs associated with constant media attention, telling the narrative of a woman's fraudulent claims over the paternity of a child. Jackson's vocal delivery and the unique bassline heighten the song's emotional intensity.

Among the heartbreaking environmental anthems produced in 1995, "Earth Song" stands out. The lyrics issue a strong call to action by addressing environmental issues and human responsibility. The song's emotional effect is amplified by Michael's vocal delivery and a dramatic orchestral arrangement, which transforms it into a powerful call for change and worldwide awareness.

Michael adopts a sympathetic narrator persona in "Heal the World," tackling societal concerns and inspiring listeners to have a positive impact on the world. The song's lyrics, which call on people to band together in order to use love and compassion to repair the planet, are empathetic and hopeful.

Although a lot of Michael Jackson's songs have a lively, danceable vibe to them, his poignant lyrics show that he was a diverse artist who used his position to address difficult subjects. Michael's literary ability brought layers of depth to his songs, striking a deep emotional chord with his followers whether he was addressing societal concerns, personal hardships, or calling for positive change.

CHAPTER 12

Reflections by Moonlight

An Examination of Michael's Songwriting Legacy in Lyrics
"Legacy in Lyrics: Analyzing Michael's Songwriting of Michael Jackson"

Often referred to as the "King of Pop," Michael Jackson had a lasting impression on the music business with both his amazing songwriting and captivating performances. His skill as an artist is shown by his ability to write songs that millions of people across the globe could relate to.

The ageless quality of Michael Jackson's lyrics is one of their most distinctive features. His songs continue to resonate with audiences of all ages, whether they deal with love, societal concerns, or personal experiences. Consider his well-known song "Billie Jean." Michael's acute grasp of the complexity of human relationships is reflected in the song's theme concerning false charges and the repercussions of erroneous gossip. The story's emotional depth is evoked in listeners by the lyrics, which also exude sincerity and a feeling of urgency.

The ability of Michael to include social criticism into his songs is another facet of his musical talent. He tackles social themes in songs like "Man in the Mirror" and "They Don't Care About Us," pushing for constructive change and questioning the present quo. These compositions demonstrate his dedication to leveraging his platform for social good, using the expressive power of words to motivate others to take action.

Notable is also the variety of themes that Michael's lyrics cover. From the reflective introspection of "Stranger in Moscow" to the ethereal romanticism of "Human Nature," his compositions span a broad spectrum of subjects. This range of topics demonstrates Michael's aptitude for delving into all facets of the human experience, resulting in a discography that is a rich tapestry of emotions.

Furthermore, Michael Jackson often used complex wordplay and deft wording in his songs. Songs like "The Way You Make Me Feel" and "Rock with You" are prime examples of his ability to communicate complicated emotions in a straightforward way. These songs display Michael's skillful use of language to build lyrics that transport listeners to rich, emotional settings.

In terms of legacy, Michael's songs still serve as an inspiration to musicians today. The fact that performers from a variety of genres have been influenced by him shows how his poetry has endured throughout the world of music. Michael's lyrics possess a timeless character that is defined by their lyrical sensibility, universal topics, and rigorous attention to detail.

Michael Jackson's songwriting is a complex examination of the human condition characterized by wordplay that is superb, social conscience, variety in subjects, and everlasting themes. His lyrics are living proof of his extraordinary genius and keep drawing crowds from all over the globe, guaranteeing that his legacy endures thanks to the everlasting force of his words.

Moonwalk in Literature: The Influence of Michael on Books and Society

"Moonwalk in Literature: Michael's Impact on Books and Culture of Michael Jackson"

Michael Jackson has had a significant impact on popular culture and literature in addition to music. Michael's autobiography, "Moonwalk," is a noteworthy example of his influence on literature and popular culture.

The 1988 book "Moonwalk" offers a close-up view of Michael Jackson's life, from his formative years with the Jackson 5 to his extraordinary solo career. The book highlights Michael's experiences, difficulties, and victories while providing readers and followers with a unique look behind the scenes of celebrity. In addition to exploring the nuances of his musical career, the book offers insights into his challenges and the effects of international fame on his life.

A noteworthy feature of "Moonwalk" is its role in dismantling prejudices and racial barriers. In an industry dominated by white people, African American musician Michael Jackson attained extraordinary success. His autobiography is a story of resiliency that highlights his will to triumph above racial discrimination and society's expectations. Readers may relate to this part of the novel since it depicts both the larger cultural changes of that time period as well as Michael's journey.

How "Moonwalk" explores creativity and creative expression only serves to enhance its cultural influence. In addition to being a pioneer in music, Michael Jackson also had a vision in other fields, including dance, fashion, and visual storytelling. The book offers a glimpse into his creative process and highlights the painstaking attention to detail that went into making his well-known music videos and live performances. Numerous artists from a variety of fields have been influenced by this creative mindset, which has shaped popular culture.

"Moonwalk" also functions as a cultural relic that advances knowledge of celebrity culture and the influence of the media on public opinion. Michael provides insightful observations on the difficulties experienced by celebrities via his interactions with the media, his thoughts on the cost of fame, and his attempts to maintain his normality in the face of severe scrutiny.

Michael Jackson's influence on literature goes beyond the pages of "Moonwalk," as seen by the many biographies, scholarly studies, and cultural commentary devoted to his life and legacy. His character has been the subject of several investigations by writers and academics who have looked at his impact on dance, fashion, music, and public attitudes. The discussion of Michael's cultural relevance and long influence is aided by these literary works.

As a key piece of Michael Jackson's cultural heritage, "Moonwalk" offers insight into the lives of one of the most recognizable people in music history. The book has an impact on conversations about race, creativity, celebrity, and the wider cultural effects of a worldwide superstar, in addition to its material. Michael Jackson's legacy has a lasting effect on literature because his life narrative encourages constant investigation and analysis in the fields of popular culture, academia, and biography.

Reexamining Neverland: Documentaries and Posthumous Narratives

"Revisiting Neverland: Posthumous Narratives and Documentaries of Michael Jackson"

Documentaries and posthumous stories about Michael Jackson's life and legacy have been widely available and hotly debated. The documentary "Leaving Neverland," which debuted in 2019, is among the most noteworthy. Under the direction of Dan Reed, the movie investigates the claims of sexual assault made by Wade Robson and James Safechuck, two people who say they were abused by Jackson as children.

"Leaving Neverland" caused a great deal of controversy and polarized views in society. Michael Jackson's defenders contend, on the one hand, that the documentary is biased and ignores the dearth of hard data to back up the claims. However, some who support the accusations contend that the movie clarifies the alleged wrongdoings and advances a larger discussion about the difficulties associated with idolizing prominent personalities.

Square One: Michael Jackson is a counter-documentary that the Jackson estate made in reaction to the controversy surrounding "Leaving Neverland." The 2019 documentary "Leaving Neverland" questions the veracity of Robson and Safechuck claims and tries to refute them. Michael Jackson was falsely accused, according to the Jackson estate, family, and fans, and his enormous contributions to the music business have been eclipsed by the scandals surrounding his life.

In addition to these films, a number of postmortem narratives have surfaced with the goal of providing a more impartial assessment of Michael Jackson's life. Some don't focus only on the disputes; they also discuss his ascent to prominence, musical brilliance, and cultural influence. These accounts often highlight the difficulties Jackson had throughout his career, such as negative media coverage, court cases, and personal hardships.

The 2016 documentary "Michael Jackson's Journey from Motown to Off the Wall" by Spike Lee is one example of this kind of story. With a focus on Jackson's formative years and artistic development, the movie offers a more joyous and complex portrait of the pop phenomenon. It displays his creative development, inventiveness, and the obstacles he surmounted to become a worldwide celebrity.

In addition, the 2020 documentary "On the Record: Michael Jackson" combines interviews with close friends, family members, and business insiders to provide a thorough analysis of the performer's life. The goal of this documentary is to give viewers a more complete picture of Michael Jackson by recognizing both his accomplishments and the scandals that surrounded him.

The effects of the accusations made against Michael Jackson, as well as the artist's legacy and personal life, have become hot topics of debate in response to the posthumous narratives and films about him. These films' many points of view illustrate how complicated Michael Jackson's life was, and viewers are left to consider how to keep the musician apart from the issues that have shaped his reputation even after his death.

Life Guidance

"Greetings and salutations from the fascinating world of Michael Jackson biography! You're going to take on the roles of a world-famous figure, a musical prodigy, and a guy whose life narrative is just as remarkable as the moonwalk itself as you begin this literary adventure.

Imagine this: every page flip will take you back to the energetic streets of Gary, Indiana, where young Michael first fell in love with music and launched an illustrious career. As the Jackson 5 mesmerizes audiences, you'll be a fly on the wall, seeing firsthand how a quiet young talent developed into the dynamic force that would forever alter the pop music landscape.

However, our journey continues beyond the flashing stage lights. We'll delve into the mysterious character of the King of Pop, a guy consumed by an unquenchable creative energy, fame's dangers, and desire. You will discover the facets of Michael Jackson's life that have contributed to his status as a cultural icon in addition to his status as a musician via the highs and lows, victories and losses.

So grab a seat, and get ready for a journey through the melodies of a life spent in the limelight, the rhythms of his classic records, and the rhythm of his innovative dance skills. Prepare to be enthralled by the music, mystique, and magic that characterized Michael Jackson. Now is the start of your journey; flip the page and let the story take you there!

Made in the USA
Columbia, SC
27 November 2024